Also by Sudhir Venkatesh

Floating City

Gang Leader for a Day

Off the Books

American Project

Youth, Globalization, and the Law

Rival Teenagers,
Their Race for a Gun,
and a Community
United to Save Them

THE TOMORROW GAME

SUDHIR VENKATESH

SIMON & SCHUSTER

NEW YORK   LONDON   TORONTO   SYDNEY   NEW DELHI

Simon & Schuster
1230 Avenue of the Americas
New York, NY 10020

First Simon & Schuster hardcover edition June 2022

SIMON & SCHUSTER and colophon are registered
trademarks of Simon & Schuster, Inc.

For information about special discounts for bulk purchases,
please contact Simon & Schuster Special Sales at 1-866-506-1949
or business@simonandschuster.com.

The Simon & Schuster Speakers Bureau can bring authors
to your live event. For more information or to book an event,
contact the Simon & Schuster Speakers Bureau at 1-866-248-3049
or visit our website at www.simonspeakers.com.

Interior design by Lewelin Polanco

Manufactured in the United States of America

10 9 8 7 6 5 4 3 2 1

Library of Congress Control Number: 2022933974

ISBN 978-1-5011-9439-9
ISBN 978-1-5011-9440-5 (ebook)

To Theodore and Violet

Truly landlocked people know they are. Know . . . that they must content themselves with bank, shore, beach because they cannot claim a coast. And having none, seldom dream of flight. But the people living in the Great Lakes region are confused by their place on the country's edge — an edge that is border but not coast. They seem to be able to live a long time believing, as coastal people do, that they are at the frontier where final exit and total escape are the only journeys left. But those five Great Lakes which the St. Lawrence feeds with memories of the sea are themselves landlocked, in spite of the wandering river that connects them to the Atlantic. Once the people of the lake region discover this, the longing to leave becomes acute, and a break from the area, therefore, is necessarily dream-bitten, but necessary nonetheless.

—TONI MORRISON, *SONG OF SOLOMON*

Note to Reader

This is a work of narrative nonfiction. It is a true story, and names and geographic identifiers have been disguised to protect the people who participated. For more information, please consult the Author's Note on page 279.

PART 1

1

Frankie Paul sits at the clean, white picnic table. His hands are clasped in prayer and his palms are clammy with sweat. His restless feet throw squeaks up from the tile floor. He is only in the prison's visitor's room, but it is enough to make him nervous.

A guard stares Frankie down. Frankie quiets his feet. *Feels a lot like school,* he thinks to himself.

The room for the guests of inmates is stark and antiseptic. The smell is of bleach and linoleum. Only one of the white walls is decorated—a large sign hangs head high: NO SHOUTING! NO TOUCHING! NO EATING AND DRINKING! NO CELL PHONES!

Two other visitors, a Latina woman and her teenage daughter, sit silently at a similar table twenty feet away. A low-pitched alarm rattles the metal bars that crisscross the windows. Frankie looks up to see Willie escorted through a thick steel door by an armed guard. His tattooed neck, arms, and chest bulge through the bluish-gray, government-issued jumpsuit. He has been working out.

Willie walks over calmly and slides gently into the seat opposite Frankie. He looks relaxed and unbothered, but Frankie knows that his older cousin is not happy.

Willie stares back at the teenager who decided to dress up for the visit—a Chicago Bulls warm-up suit, all white, from head to toe, and a bright offsetting MJ red hat. Willie does not say anything to his cousin, except to nod that he is ready to listen.

Frankie starts off with an apology that he has been rehearsing for the past hour.

"Wasn't my fault, Willie, I did my best. We got a problem . . ." Frankie stammers. "Willie, I know you're mad— But . . . but I need need to explain something to you."

Frankie starts to perspire. His speech is halting and he is losing his breath. He struggles to finish a sentence. Then Willie raises his hands and shakes his head. Relieved, Frankie stops talking. The inmate's eyes turn steely and his nose flares. Willie has decided that today's conversation will now be a monologue.

"You shouldn't be here," he says softly. "But I do understand *why* you're here. I mean, I wish you *weren't* here, cuz, but we got to get past that, right? Is what it is."

Frankie sits back and mashes his sweaty palms together. Before leaving for prison, Willie instructed Frankie to stay away from lockup. Far away. Specifically, Willie gave orders to remain in Chicago. Frankie should only send messages via Calvin, the prison security guard who Willie's gang keeps on retainer. Willie warned Frankie that cops would be checking the visitation logs of new inmates. It is the easiest way to figure out who might be taking over the street drug trade of an incarcerated kingpin.

Over the past two months, Frankie has been using Calvin to communicate with his cousin in prison.

Calvin is happy to provide this service for Willie and other imprisoned gang leaders—the $500 per month, tax-free, is helpful given his salary is never enough to pay the bills. And, for Willie, Calvin is particularly useful since the two grew up together in Rosewood, the South Side Chicago neighborhood where Willie set up his drug business. Calvin shuttles back and forth between the downstate prison and Rosewood to transmit messages, keep tabs on Frankie, and provide general intel on happenings in Rosewood's underworld.

The most recent messages came in hot. "It's all going to shit, Willie," Calvin reported. "You got to do something." Calvin recommended that Willie step up his communication with Frankie and give him more direction on how to run a drug trafficking business. Calvin has seen this situation many times before—a newly imprisoned drug leader tries to keep control of their drug trade from behind bars. Managing from the streets is hard enough, but directing from prison is nearly impossible.

Calvin's last two updates for Willie made it clear that his seventeen-year-old cousin was failing as the crew chief. His report to Willie was simple:

"You gonna lose your business, Willie. Everything you worked for," Calvin said directly, a few days before Frankie's visit. "Niggers all around you looking to step in—take your shit. Let Frankie come down here and talk with you. Your boy ain't handling things well." That was all it took for Willie to accept Frankie's request for a face-to-face.

At the visitor's table, Frankie fidgets nervously. "I'm gonna say a few things, Frankie," Willie says firmly. "And you gonna listen. Dig? Look around. Ain't no need for you to say nothin' in this room. Dig?"

Frankie looks around and notices that the guards are watching them closely. He nods, though reluctantly. He wants his turn to speak. He needs Willie to understand just how difficult his life has become. He has never managed a gang, never sold drugs, never faced hostile competitors. Every day is new to him. He has come with a long list of questions for Willie: *How do I deal with suppliers who are getting pissed at me? How do I get my crew to listen to me? Should I be nervous about the car sitting across the street that watches us all day?*

As a rookie street manager, Frankie has been facing one stressful situation after another. It all started the day Willie announced that Frankie would be stepping in to lead the team. Hearing this, Willie's team members quit in disgust. They refused to take orders from an inexperienced teenager. And they were angry Willie didn't have enough confidence to select one of them.

Frankie ended up replacing Willie's veteran crew—each member had been around for at least a decade—with inexperienced teens, much like himself. This action only further excited the local gangs who began plotting their rival takeover. Customers also took notice, immediately heading out to find a new drug supplier—no addict wants to be caught in the middle of gang crossfire.

And, worst of all from a purely business standpoint, the sudden drop in demand made suppliers hesitant. They retreated and walked away, which meant Frankie's crew was running out of product. Willie would now need to communicate with suppliers from his prison cell. Through Calvin, he would need to send them a message his operation was secure and demand was strong.

And then came the final blow. Some local youth robbed Frankie's men in broad daylight. They laughed as they took the loot in front of a group of teenage girls who, witnessing the entire incident go down, quickly spread the news on Facebook and Twitter.

Bunch of fucking pussies!
Them bitches got what they deserved.

Hour after hour, across social media, Frankie's team suffered a virtual beatdown.

The net effect was that Willie's drug outfit, with his little cousin Frankie now in charge, was vulnerable and weak. The lucrative turf at the western border of Holden Park, the turf that Willie risked his life for so many years to retain, could soon very well be under someone else's control. The business he built up—the years he spent fighting and clawing on the streets to stay in command—was about to be taken from him.

Over the years, Willie had rightfully earned his many titles— "King," "Kingpin," "Boss," "Chief." People referred to him with each. He was now on the verge of losing it all.

With his hands resting on the picnic table, Willie is well aware he cannot focus on these disastrous outcomes. The brief meetup in the

7

visitors' room is not the place to show weakness. He does his best to find words that might soothe Frankie. "Cuz, I been where you been, I know this ain't easy. You can do this. I promise. Just remember you're dealing with *young* niggers. That ain't always easy. You dig?"

"I get it, I get it, Willie," Frankie stammers. "And I got some ideas *myself*."

Willie is in no mood to hear Frankie's ideas. He raises his hand again.

"Frankie, your team is young," he says quietly. "When a *young* nigger gets in the game, he can be confused. You're their leader and they depending on you. Dig?"

Willie chooses his words carefully. Frankie has assembled a team of boys with no street background to do the man's job of running dope 24-7. They are unfamiliar with the pressures of street trading. Frankie needs to turn them into a *team*.

Willie needs Frankie to take control and show some guts. Be a leader, not a scared teenager. Willie knows he must *inspire*.

"Right now, you need to give your crew someone to fight, got it? Find someone who wants to see your boys get hurt, be dead, or worse—*flat fucking broke*. Every soldier got to have an enemy or he ain't a soldier. It's that simple. Dig? You need to start hunting someone down. Find an enemy! *Now!* You dig?"

Willie pounds his fist into the table. The visitors and guards turn around abruptly. He motions to the guard that he is ready to return to his cell. He has heard enough. He nods at Frankie—a final note of encouragement.

Frankie looks up at Willie as he leaves the room and the door clangs behind him. All he wishes for is to return home and curl up in bed. He wants his former life back—the one that did not involve directing a complex drug trafficking operation. He wants Willie to be the supportive and wise older cousin, the nurturing family member who looked out for him.

Not his boss.

Ten minutes later, Frankie sits alone in his car, in the middle of the larger of two parking lots for visitors. He stares up at the prison, expecting to see Willie looking down at him from the thin window slits that break up the concrete and steel wall. He lights and discards one Newport after another and combs through Willie's words for meaning as the song on the stereo gathers force. Tupac's voice soothes him. Frankie closes his eyes and loses himself in the lyrics.

I bet you got it twisted, you don't know who to trust. So many player-hatin' niggas tryna sound like us.

Frankie reminds himself how far he has come. He tells himself to be proud of his progress. The world changed abruptly after his mother died from cancer over a year ago. Frankie moved from relative to relative. For a stretch, he was shuttled off to foster care. The constant move from family to family left him fragile and depressed. New schools, new gang boundaries, new friends and foes. The experience put him in a perpetual rut, anxious and moody, and without hope. Each morning, he woke up scared and in a pool of sweat. He could barely get out of bed.

It was Willie who came to the rescue. Didn't matter that his old cousin could only offer Frankie an old, tattered mattress. It was family. It felt good to be at Willie's side.

Frankie spent his days working menial side jobs for Willie's drug crew. He didn't mind running errands, washing cars, or going to the corner store to buy extra condoms when the sex workers arrived for the weekend poker parties. He didn't even mind that he was living in a house that was used primarily for storing drugs, guns, and cash. Willie had purchased the home in his aunt's name with his drug receipts. According to the state, Willie's aunt, who had never set foot in the place, was Frankie's guardian. None of this mattered. Willie made Frankie feel needed. Loved. He could stay there forever.

Eventually, Willie taught him things. Useful things like how to package dope, how to hire a homeless man for daily chores, like hiding cash or picking up lunch for the crew. Willie would challenge Frankie by giving him new tasks. Frankie relished the apprenticeship. No one had showed such care since Mom passed away. After a few months, Frankie casually mentioned to Willie that he quit school. He informed the Boss he was now devoted 100 percent to the cause. Frankie may not have found his calling, but at least he was out of foster care, thank the Lord. And he was happy.

Then came Willie's arrest. Willie knew he'd made a mistake purchasing twenty handguns from an out-of-town trader. The buy was large enough to attract the attention of a surveilling undercover police unit. Cops will let you run a little dope and they may even look the other way for a purchase of a few guns. Willie knew that. But if you go big—guns, drugs, money laundering—you're screwed. No neighborhood cop wants someone hanging around with so much power.

Once again, after Willie's arrest, Frankie felt the world crumble around him. He feared that he would return to foster care.

"You gonna be okay, cuz. Everyone been doing this for a long time, so you just gotta let them do their thing. Got it? Don't try to do something *different*. No one expecting you to do that. Dig? You keep it easy, and you gonna be with me for a long time."

How bad could it really be? Frankie thought. Willie promised the five-year sentence would be shortened to three years for good behavior. Frankie wasn't paying much attention. The crew was trained. The day-to-day work was one routine after another. The business looked to be on autopilot. Leading the team would be straightforward.

Things unraveled right away. Nothing went right after Willie told his men that Frankie was the new boss. His orders were met with laughter and some days no one showed up for work. Frankie couldn't understand why. It seemed like such a small change. *Just keep doing what you are doing*, Willie told the team. Frankie repeated it. But no one listened. In fact, they soon rebelled. Crew members, most in their twenties and thirties, stole product, hid cash, played with the numbers and, when nothing was left to pilfer, they walked away. There was little chance a teenager would be their boss.

What happened to the old days, Frankie kept asking himself, when gang loyalties were said to pass from father to son—when even the thought of exiting could earn you a severe beating?

Frankie assembled a new crew, a five-person outfit—three scrappy ex-athletes who'd been kicked off the football team and two more from a foster care home where Frankie had once lived. He found them, recruited them, and assigned them each a role in the gang. But once again, he was alone, overwhelmed and without a trusted adult whom he could lean on for guidance. No surprise that the frightening thought crept into his head: *Maybe going back to foster care would be better for me?* This is not a thought Frankie likes to acknowledge. Whenever it rises, he pushes it away. Foster care is endless misery, a cycle of new homes with new rules, and one low-income neighborhood after another where he was alone and afraid to walk the streets for fear of being beaten or recruited by local gangs.

Frankie feels stuck. Street thugging or cycling through unfamiliar foster care families. Both feel like forms of punishment.

There's got to be a way out, Frankie thinks to himself.

As the song concludes, Frankie opens his eyes and looks around. People are staring at the thumping, swaying car. Frankie wants to sob. He wants the relief of letting out a long wail. He rolls down the car window, lights another cigarette, and gathers himself.

He does his best to take some comfort from the visit with Willie. *Find an enemy. Find an enemy.* Willie's words ring in his ears.

Frankie starts laughing out loud. *Is it really so simple?* he wonders.

At that moment, Frankie realizes that Willie has given him a way out. These three words are his path to freedom. Frankie whispers them over and over until his grimace breaks into a soft smile. *Find an enemy.* He shakes his head and laughs at himself. *Why didn't I think of this before?!* he mutters to himself.

Frankie pulls out of the prison parking lot and drives off northward, back toward Chicago and his Rosewood neighborhood. As he speeds past the cars on the two-lane highway, he does a mental survey of his Rosewood community back in Chicago. He comes up with other gangs and crews who are his likely competitors—Vice Lords, 88th St. Disciples, Black Devils. A few occupy neighboring territories, while some are based miles away. He settles on a half dozen who seem intent on trying to take over his operation.

He doesn't know these people. None of these half-dozen intruders feels like an *enemy*. And, even if they were, they frighten him. Each is led by a far more experienced leader. Frankie knows he will be hurt or killed if he puts up any resistance.

What the hell is an enemy, anyway? he wonders.

Swerving across several lanes of traffic, Frankie exits and drives into a convenience store parking lot. He leaves the engine running, skips in and out of the store, and drops three Mountain Dews and a bag of donuts on the seat.

An enemy is someone you hate, right? But, who do I really hate? I know I hate somebody.

Frankie smiles and grabs his cell phone.

"Better tell Antoine," he mutters. Antoine is his trusted lieutenant, his best friend, and the smartest person he knows. And, though Antoine also never ran drugs, Frankie finds him to be sensible and capable of making good decisions.

When Antoine answers, Frankie blurts out. "Antoine! Listen! Got to do it. We need a meeting! Call a meeting, now! We got work to do. We're going after the *enemy*."

Two hundred miles away, back in Rosewood, Antoine struggles to keep up. Frankie's shouting catches him off guard. The cold September wind makes it difficult to catch every word of Frankie's shouting. Antoine can't recall Frankie mentioning that he would be heading downstate to see Willie. Antoine tries to slow Frankie down, pressing him to give up details about the visit.

"What did Willie say?" Antoine wants to know.

"Don't worry," Frankie says. "Let's meet at the Lake in a few hours. I'm driving back. Just do what I say. Get everyone together."

"For what?" Antoine asks incredulously. "People gonna ask me what we meeting about. It ain't time for our weekly. So, what's the big deal?!"

"We're going after someone! We're gonna go after Marshall Mariot! We gonna take that nigger down!"

2

While Frankie visits Willie in prison, Marshall Mariot begins his Monday morning with a mile-long walk to school. Nowadays every walk makes him nervous. A part of him expects to confront Frankie Paul's crew at any moment.

Fucking Frankie Paul, Marshall thinks.

He avoids the gangs. He is never in trouble with the police. He works short stints at the strip mall retailers. And he is rarely truant at school, even if his C average does not win him high praise from teachers.

Marshall has never been ambitious. And where does ambition get the teenager in Rosewood anyway? Occasionally, one hears of an academic achiever and gifted athlete. But families usually whisk these rarities off to smaller cities—Iowa City, Kalamazoo, St. Paul—where they live with relatives who cultivate their talents. Since they do not return, they are easily forgotten. Ambitious youth who hang around are visible, but they are into gangbanging and the underworld. This means they usually end up in prison or the mortuary, which makes perseverance and dedication notable virtues, but hardly enough to help you live the clean life.

Earlier this year, everything changed for Marshall. His plan to enjoy life as a seventeen-year-old—and especially his last summer before senior year—was shot down. Parents, school counselors and teachers, relatives—even Grandma—pestered him with questions about his "plans." *When will you be leaving home? What's your chosen career? How are you going to support yourself?* Marshall wanted to put on headphones and turn it all off. He wanted to tell them what he was *really* thinking. *I like my room. Why do I need to leave home? Why can't I live here for a while?!* But each time he started to speak anger got the best of him. He felt asthmatic, with no room to breathe. So he shut his mouth and let things be.

Then there was *Fucking Frankie Paul.*

All that taunting after school. The pushing and needling at the Chicken Shack at lunch. And right in front of the girls! The entire history of his dealings with Frankie Paul plays out like a horror movie in his mind. He fixates on one incident with the bully. It was late summer—a month ago. His friends were on their way to Holden Park, where the Boys and Girls Club sponsored a youth talent show. Together with Georgie and Siron, Marshall was about to perform a rap song for the crowd—an old Dr. Dre throwback.

Frankie stopped the group on their walk to the club. In the middle of the sidewalk, with some neighborhood girls watching, Frankie went after Marshall with taunts. "Yo! Babyface!" Frankie chided Marshall. He then threatened to pee all over Marshall's backpack. Everyone was staring. Marshall wanted to disappear.

But he didn't. Instead, he went after Frankie. Marshall instinctively lunged at Frankie and wrestled him to the ground. So far, so good, but when the two were back on their feet, Marshall's balance was off. He lunged forward to throw a punch, but it missed, and Marshall tripped over himself and spun pathetically to the ground. More shame and more public ridiculing followed. Might as well be silent was the lesson Marshall took away. But that just brought on more friction. This wasn't junior high, where the bullies moved on to play with a better toy. No, a week later, another encounter with Frankie's crew in Holden Park. They shook up bottles of Miller Lite and splattered Marshall's group before laughing hysterically and running off.

Now Marshall regularly changes his route to school, taking a new alley or side street in an effort to hide from Frankie. This morning, with his jaw tight and his eyes constantly peering about, he walks briskly and scans the horizon. He sprints past a short, open stretch of train tracks strewn with condoms, cigarette packages, and beer cans. The adrenaline rushes through him.

Today, there is a stop along the way—the vacant three-story brownstone at the northern border of Holden Park. The century-old brownstone, where Marshall's grandparents once lived, sits across the park, from where Frankie Paul's crew is based. It is also the place where Marshall was born. When Grandpa died a few years later, Grandma moved in with Marshall's family; and the landlord who moved out of the city just let the brownstone grow vacant. The front stoop had been a refuge, a stop for Marshall to strike up a conversation with Grandpa, and to escape from his own family drama and hide from the pressures of daily life. Today, Marshall's friends join him there. The teens huddle next to one another, sitting close to shelter themselves from the wind.

Marshall slowly makes his way up the eleven plaster and stone stairs, all the way to the semicircular stoop that rings the front porch. His friends' heads buried into the Facebook and Twitter feeds that flash across their phones.

Marshall is sleepy, tired, and anxious from weeks of dealing with Frankie. These friends are his best shot at finding a path out of his troubles. He sets his backpack down and peers across the park. From this perch, he can see clear almost to the other side, far past the joggers and the chess players, past the feeders at the duck pond, and clear across to the baseball fields where a small group is playing softball. If it weren't for a clump of oak trees and brush at the edge of the pond, he would have a clear view of Frankie Paul and his crew.

One good thing has come out of this for Marshall. Frankie's bullying is now officially an intergroup conflict. Marshall has friends he could turn to. Marshall and his friends couldn't be more different from Frankie's crew. Marshall's friends play video games after school, while Frankie's crew sells bags of weed near the park. Marshall likes to ride mountain bikes with his friends, while Frankie just paid $6,000 for two stolen cars. One thinks about acne, the other is stocking up on large parcels of marijuana.

Fucking Frankie Paul, Marshall thinks. *I'd love to get back at him.*

———————

Today, Marshall will make a plea to his friends: he wants to go after that bully Frankie, and he wants them to join him.

Just as Marshall's about to ask the boys, they hear sputtering muffler sounds and creaking mettle. A van speeds arounds the corner, hopping over the curb in reckless flight. A screech, a sudden stop, and a door flying open. These sounds announce a thirtysomething man who jumps out and lights a cigarette as he marches over to the group.

It is Jonny Isaac. Hustler, con artist, "Old Head" in Rosewood, Jonny is known to one and all in the community. In Jonny, many young boys will see their future. Most of the older residents look at Jonny with a mixture of pity and disgust—he is an easy mark for parents who need to provide an example of why it pays to stay in school and get a job. But, for the younger set, Jonny is a badass, seemingly always on the verge of something risky and exciting.

"Here we go!" Jonny shouts, as he walks up the stairs, catching everyone off guard. Marshall's friend Siron invited Jonny, thinking that the hustler could give the group a few ideas to beat back Frankie and his crew. Knowing Marshall and his friends might be hesitant to speak with him, Jonny encouraged Siron to keep his visit a surprise.

Jonny takes a moment to adjust his jacket—a worn, black leather waist-length coat, with silver buttons and ornate stitching across the shoulders and back. His long, flared jeans and shiny loafers make a gentle noise—*whoosh, tap, whoosh, tap*—as he moves back and forth on the stoop in front of Marshall and his friends. He opens up his presentation in a teacherly way. In his hands is a .44 Magnum pistol that he slides through the thick autumn air slowly and deliberately. He passes the gun in front of Marshall's face and then steps past the others. He twirls the cylinder around to ensure that every teen has a view.

Jonny quickly points the gun up and looks everyone in the eye. "If you want to scare them boys, this will do it. Show them this beast and they'll run! You'll never have no trouble no more."

He smiles, turns the weapon around and presents the handle to Marshall, daring him to grab hold. Marshall wants no part of it. The gun frightens him. He has never fired a weapon nor held one for more than a few seconds. He shakes his head and looks away.

"That's cool," Jonny chides Marshall. "No big thing. If you ain't ready, you ain't ready." He turns his back to Marshall and addresses the others. No one can take their eyes off the revolver. Clean and shiny, with an inviting blackness. They are transfixed.

"Let me hold it," Georgie smiles nervously as he reaches for the gun. He looks over at Marshall. He knows his best friend would rather that he not play along. But the chance to hold the gun is too good to pass up. He wraps his hands around the handle. He struggles to control the weight. He nearly drops the piece on the ground. The others laugh and slap high fives.

Marshall frowns, but no one pays him any mind. Everyone gets ready for their turn. One by one, they stand up and delicately grab hold of Jonny's showpiece. They run their fingers and palms over the smooth metal. Some point the barrel farther down the street toward the row of decaying gray brownstones. Siron tucks it into the side of his pants, as though into a holster, and pulling it back out quickly, he pretends to pick off a makeshift target with the gun at his hips. The others hoot and holler, egging each other on.

Jonny knows that this is now *his* crowd. He continues with his performance, ignoring Marshall. He grabs the revolver, and then turns his body around, making eye contact with each of the boys.

"Okay, let's go over a few things," Jonny says. "What's this part?" He points at the chamber. No one answers. "Okay, how do you load this baby? Where you gonna get bullets? What do you do when you ain't using it . . . ?"

Jonny stops abruptly. The quizzing tells him exactly what he needed to know. The group is inexperienced and intimidated—which gives him an opportunity to make a buck.

"This is a man's gun." Jonny smiles. The boys can see that he has his own special bond with the weapon. "I'm going to help you learn how to take care of yourself. And I might give you a special price for that. We can talk about that later. But let me tell you that I was a young buck, like you. I know what it's like to defend yourself. You dig?"

Jonny has given this speech many times before, and to many different audiences. He is comfortable among the wide range of desperate and scared persons in Rosewood. He speaks with equal passion to the addict looking for a quick source of protection, the burglar in search of just the right pick for an available lock, the prostitute needing to confront an abusive john, and the teenager needing to take a stand and recapture pride. Indeed, for anyone in Rosewood needing to settle a score, find something illegal, or initiate a scam, Jonny Isaac is the go-to resource. He and his van—a roving black market—are open and ready to serve.

Jonny knows Marshall and his friends have come to the stoop to discuss their suffering at the hands of a local bully. They are afraid, desperate, and in need of a solution. They are just the right kind of client. The group of boys appeals to Jonny's strengths.

The average adult in the community knows to call bullshit on Jonny's tall tales. No one in Rosewood is convinced by his boasting and exaggerated claims. They roll their eyes, laugh, and move on when Jonny whips up some speech about his bravado. But not teenagers, who become wide-eyed in Jonny's presence. The hustler's swagger is what they want to feel—his testimonials are what they need to hear to become *men*. For the young and uninitiated, Jonny is like something out the Wild West: a fearless and fiercely independent hero with money in his pocket, a working vehicle that serves as his roving office, and an endless stream of entertaining stories. Jonny knows everyone, so it is worthwhile knowing him.

For today's sales pitch, Jonny is offering up his old standby: the large Magnum his own father gave him the night he died. In reality, the weapon is just teen bait—an opening act. Jonny knows Marshall and his friends cannot afford the $2,500 purchase price. No matter. If everything goes well, the performance will win him a second meeting, at which point he will offer up a less costly and more practical firearm. It is all part of a tried-and-true script Jonny has honed for teens who are being shamed, insulted, and harassed, and need to recover their dignity in the neighborhood. Get them armed for a reasonable price so they can restore their manhood.

It is the honor game and Jonny is a seasoned player.

Jonny stares at the lost boys and ratchets up his sales pitch. "I know y'all are about to check somebody. Am I right?"

"If you're going after that boy, then you need to be ready. Can't be playing around like no shorties no more. It's time to be *men*. What do you think? You ready for one of these? *You ready to be men?*"

The young men stare at Jonny, who is holding up the gun under the lamppost light. They glance over to one other. *Were they ready?*

"*That* boy will be ready, don't you worry," Jonny continues. "You ain't gonna surprise him just by coming up on him."

Jonny pushes the gun up in the air. "But, if you bring this out. Yeah, you bring *this* out! *Oooh!* He'll take you seriously."

Marshall looks away and scans his friends. They are spellbound.

"I didn't ask you to come, Jonny." Marshall stands up. He needs to put Jonny in his place. He does his best to interrupt Jonny, but his heart is racing and his delivery is shaky. Jonny says nothing and just stares at Marshall, who quickly quiets down and takes a seat.

Marshall crams his quaking hands into his coat pockets. This was supposed to be his moment in the spotlight. Today was the day he would be delivering an impassioned speech to the group. He would be leading them into battle against their bully. It was his time to shine. Now Marshall feels it all slipping away.

Jonny looks at the group and expresses disappointment. "Hey, I thought you was serious," he says. He stuffs the gun down the front of his trousers. "If you all wasn't serious, you shouldn't have told me to come. I got better things to do."

Jonny walks closer to his cousin, Siron, who is sitting a few feet away from Marshall. Siron stands up and delivers his own plea in support of his older cousin. "Man, we got to listen to Jonny. You really think these niggers are going to leave us alone just because we *ask* them to? Fuck no! We need to show them we ain't taking their shit no more!"

"Cuz is right," Jonny says, taking out the gun once again. "You ain't even got to load this bitch. Leave the bullets at home! But, like I said, you show it one time? You ain't never gonna have no more trouble with those little bitches again. Guaranteed!"

Siron and Jonny laugh and shake hands. Jonny's work is done. He will now let the group stew a bit. He lights a cigarette and leads Siron down the sidewalk. They stop at a rusted-out Lincoln Town Car taking up half the side yard. They check phones and exchange puffs of a Newport.

Marshall stares at his closest friend, Georgie. Sensing Marshall is dejected, Georgie reminds everyone why they have gathered.

"Yo! We ain't gonna take it no more," Georgie stands up and cries out. "You hear me! We need to do something together. All of us, together. They keep coming after us because we ain't fought back. I say we do what Marshall says. Go over there on the weekend and take care of them niggers."

Silence. Jonny and his revolver still loom over them. Not because it is bigger and more daunting than the beat-up pistols that populate their neighborhood. And not because it is the first gun they have seen or touched. No, there are guns in the homes of family members. But this one feels magical. It seems to have arrived just when they asked for help.

For the past two weeks, Marshall and Georgie had carefully developed a strategy to confront Frankie Paul: First, they'd convene their friends on the stoop. Then Georgie would appoint Marshall as their leader, and everyone would vow to join forces. Finally, they'd head over to meet the bully and fight for their manhood. And just like that they would win back their senior year of high school!

Instead, they got Jonny Isaac. Jonny, the son of an imprisoned gang leader who himself had spent ten years behind bars. Jonny, the crafty son of a bitch who saw every ghetto passerby as his mark. Survival by parasite. Jonny was damn good at that.

Jonny walks back to his van, opens a creaky door, jumps inside, and lowers his window. Throwing out a cigarette, he drives away slowly. Siron decides not to rejoin the boys on the stoop, and he walks off. Marshall's friends look dazed and confused. It is unclear whether Georgie's speech has landed. It is late. Everyone is weary and rattled.

Jonny's question hangs in the air: *Were they ready?*

"Hey! We can do this!" Georgie stands up. He knows he needs

to close the meeting. They are already late for school. He needs everyone to focus on the task at hand. "Maybe Jonny can help us. Maybe not. But, we got to make a plan. We said we was gonna work together, so let's do it. Marshall and I will figure some shit out. Okay?"

The group agrees to meet later that afternoon. As people drift away, Georgie comforts Marshall.

"You alright? Don't worry about Siron. I didn't know that brother was going to bring Jonny with him today. I'll talk to Siron later. He's with us."

Marshall does not respond.

"Maybe Jonny and Siron are right," Georgie continues. "If we want to stop that boy, we gonna need to carry *something*."

"Maybe," says Marshall. He stands up and walks down the stoop. "All I know is *that boy* ain't gonna fuck with us no more. I'm going after him."

"True. We gonna get him for sure!" Georgie shouts. The two friends walk down the stoop. They decide to leave school as early as possible and strategize back at Marshall's bedroom—their unofficial war room.

3

Antoine Cardoza Wilson, aka Antoine T, was born at the Rosewood Community Clinic to a mother who was beaten up by her boyfriend the night of the birth. His only prized possession is a small photo of his mother taken by a nurse minutes after Antoine was born: Momma, aka Princess Wilson, with left eye black-and-blue, a tooth knocked out, and cheeks inflamed by contact with a man's fist, is smiling as she holds her newly arrived son in her arms.

Antoine looks at that photo every morning and prays. He promises to be a better man for his momma. Every day he promises to do better than the day before. This morning, he stared at the photo for several minutes after Frankie called him. Frankie's announcement that they would be going after Marshall Mariot has left him confused and frustrated. *Why Marshall?* Antoine wonders. Each time Frankie comes up with an idea, something is likely to go wrong. Monday isn't half over, and Frankie is already stirring up shit.

Slowly dragging himself out of the house, he puts on a jacket and heads over to the lakefront, where the rest of the crew will be meeting.

Of late, Antoine has been praying for some help at his uncle Albert's place of worship—a storefront sanctuary on Rosewood's western border. After Princess was hospitalized with her third heroin overdose, Uncle Albert took up the role of project manager for Antoine's life. Three times a week, Antoine and Uncle Albert review the work ahead, assess progress, set intentions, and create the necessary focus so that Antoine can leave his neighborhood. They need him to get on with his life, which means getting out of Rosewood.

Valparaiso University, Indiana. That is their destination. Antoine's father and Uncle Albert both attended, though neither ended up graduating. Albert intends on keeping that tradition alive with his nephew. Uncle Albert promised his Maker that Antoine would not waste his life on the streets of Chicago. He vows to drop him off at Valparaiso to start classes the following year.

Antoine is on board with the plan. He never wanted to be in a gang. He doesn't like fighting and he can't stand selling drugs. He wants out of the ghetto. Fast.

But without a father and with Momma at home battling late-stage cancer, Antoine is struggling. Joining Frankie's crew has given him an unexpected lifeline. Antoine declined Frankie's offer for months. But soon, the meager drug income became an attractive means to pay rent until Momma was healthy again.

Uncle Albert thought hard about Antoine's decision to join Frankie's crew. Albert initially did not approve. But he knows that Antoine is fiercely independent and wants the feeling that he is supporting his mother. Albert can sense that Antoine has made up his mind. And they both agree that running with Frankie will probably be for a year at most, so Albert doesn't push his disapproval. At least Antoine would be close by in Rosewood where he could be watched.

Albert is himself no stranger to the wayward path. Twenty years ago, when he returned from college, he decided to run with a gun trafficking crew. A stretch in prison, then on the street selling drugs and more prison time followed. On his third stint behind bars, Albert found a new cellmate: the Lord. He walked out clean and sober, and straight into the seminary.

In the local community of clergy, Albert proudly sees himself in an outcast role. On one side, there are a dozen prominent clergy in Rosewood, each of whom is well known throughout Chicago's South Side Black community and beyond. They have steady membership, which means plenty of money and part-time help to keep their churches well maintained. With plenty of clout, they can bring out the vote for local candidates. None of these preachers welcome Albert in their fold. Albert lacks a stable of wealthier out-of-town families. The donations from his congregants are meager, inconsistent, and usually arrive in the form of crumpled-up bills instead of checks and wire transfers. Albert will never be called by city leaders who can channel pots of money to his church for consulting, social services, and youth programming. His church is on a modest lot, with no separate parking and no landscaping. In between weekend services, Albert is an active handyman and a construction worker. He hustles to pay the bills. He knows what Antoine wakes up to every day.

This places Albert in the company of another class of local preachers, one with a different type of clout in Rosewood. At the top of this small group is Albert's friend whose well-decorated house of worship sits just a few blocks away. Pastor Jesse is the leader of a group of self-described "street elders" whose power comes from their ability to keep the streets safe — or at least resolve problems before they get out of hand. Pastor Jesse is the one whom the gang leaders turn to for help. He creates truces among warring drug crews, and, in the case of Antoine, he is the likely person Albert will call if Antoine gets himself in trouble.

All of this is on Albert's mind as he considers Antoine's work with Frankie's crew. Albert has not yet called on Pastor Jesse or the other elders, but he has sought counsel from the Lord. He asked his Maker, *Should my nephew really take up this opportunity to earn dirty money?* What Albert came away with, to his own surprise, was that the Lord entertained a more complicated picture of ghetto life.

Albert shared with Antoine the Lord's view on the matter. "God told me something, Antoine. He don't bring you opportunities out of nowhere, see. This one is a test. You do what you have to do, and you keep talking to me every day. Maybe God wants you to see how bad it is out there. Maybe what you're supposed to do is to learn to walk away from those boys. I don't know. But you keep praying and you'll figure it out."

Uncle Albert cautions that Antoine would do well to notify him of any problems he encounters after joining up with Frankie. The basis of their agreement is simple: "Don't hide nothing from me. Got it? Anything that you think Frankie is doing that's gonna mess things up for you, I need to know. Don't let that nigger fuck up your life."

Uncle Albert's vision resonates with Antoine, who believes in signs from above. He decides to serve as Frankie's treasurer, but on one nonnegotiable condition. He tells Frankie that he will exit the gang after one year with no repercussions. This means no beating and no financial penalty. Antoine couldn't care less if he ever sees Frankie and his friends again.

"Motherfucker, I get to leave when I want, for no reason, and no one comes after me," Antoine said to Frankie at their South Side lakefront meeting spot, a thirty-minute walk from where they sold drugs in Rosewood. "No one touches me," Antoine said several times in that exchange—aware that Willie has sent his men to physically assault other members who quit in the past. Frankie happily agreed, as he was struggling to run the operation by himself. He promised Antoine he would let Willie know that Antoine could exit without fear.

So far, Antoine has done his best to honor their agreement. But Antoine has a bad feeling about his last call with Frankie. He could hear the desperation in Frankie's voice after his visit with Willie. It sounded like another of Frankie's poorly-thought-out ways of dealing with their team's struggles to run a business.

Antoine is the last to arrive at the park for the meeting. The autumn sunlight pierces through the low-hanging clouds, adding a warm glow to the gently rolling waves on Lake Michigan. An elderly Black man walks serpentine on the park grass. He is wearing headphones and passing a metal detector over the distressed, rock-strewn ground.

Four lanes of swiftly moving traffic separate Chicago's long lakefront expanse from the eastern edge of the Rosewood community where Frankie Paul's crew is based. The crew deals their illicit goods—marijuana, OxyContin and prescription drugs, coke and speed—outside a small bungalow across the street from Rosewood's Holden Park. About two years ago, Willie smartly invested 75 percent of his cash receipts into the home. He purchased it in the name of his aunt, who has never lived there. Inside, he stores cash, weapons, and drugs. But Willie encourages Frankie to hold team meetings at a separate location, and out in the open—better for team focus and easier to spot spies.

Frankie sits at the only corner of the concrete table that is not splattered with bird droppings and stale beer. He stares into the cold wind and rubs his chalky hands together. The other four crew members are joking about an upcoming sweet sixteen party. Antoine walks up with his phone pressed against his ear. He takes off his backpack and leans against the table. As soon as he puts the phone down, the complaints start.

"Antoine, I got nothing left," says sixteen-year-old Jamie, who's in charge of daytime sales. "They keep coming and asking for more. What do I do? You want me to stand out there if all I can say is *no*?!"

"Yes," Antoine says. The group cannot afford to lose hold of their sales spot. "Just tell them we getting more in a few days."

"Me too," quips Booty, the nighttime salesman who has neither pot nor coke to offer his customers. "People getting pissed, Antoine. They saying they ain't coming back if we keep running out."

"They'll come back," Antoine says. He looks everyone in the eye to provide reassurance. "Don't worry, they can't go nowhere else and get the deal we giving them. I'm working on it, alright? You niggers got to stay calm because if you look scared, they gonna know something's up."

"You want me to keep everything with me? In my house?" Booty asks. Nobody on the team feels safe holding cash or storing it at home. Somehow local street robbers always manage to figure out who is carrying money. A robbery brings about shame, and as if that wasn't bad enough, they can count on getting beat up badly during the incident.

"Yes," Antoine responds. "We ain't got no one to hold for us right now. Best to just keep everything where you live."

One by one, Antoine calmly fields team members' questions. Only after doing so does he look up at Frankie to ask, "So, what's up?"

"We got some serious shit to deal with," Frankie says. "Willie's got something we need to take care of. I'm about to tell you what *he* wants us to do, alright? What *he* says we need to do, alright? Willie told me himself. And you know that nigger knows what he's talking about. We got to stop Marshall and them boys. Fast. Before they put us out of business. Antoine and me will figure shit out, but you all need to get ready. It's on!"

No one blinks. Frankie's announcement has fallen flat. He hasn't prepared anything more to say.

The crew picks up on his discomfort. They pepper him with questions. No one understands why Marshall has suddenly become their target.

"But Marshall don't sell no product. Why we think he's coming for our business?"

"Let's just beat the nigger when he's alone—why we need to go after all of his friends?"

"Are you sure Willie wants us to go after *Marshall*? That brother don't slang dope!"

Since joining the team, Antoine has been careful to gather intel on the local gang and drug scene. He knows that keeping up with competitors and threats is a key part of staying out of trouble. Each week, Antoine goes over the names of other outfits, block by block. There are plenty of others who might come after them. The most likely is Mo-Mo—a fortysomething drug boss who has been slanging dope on Rosewood's streets since the 1990s. Mo-Mo's group has long coveted Willie's turf next to the park. It is no secret that they look at Frankie as ready to be picked off.

Marshall Mariot is a new name for Antoine. Frankie has boasted on occasion about picking on Marshall after school. Antoine knows that the other crew members joined in the fun by ribbing Marshall's friends at parties and high school football games. But Antoine believes Marshall to be a weak kid with no appetite for fighting or selling drugs. Even in the few altercations with Frankie, Marshall sounded innocent and awkward. Antoine finds it hard to believe that this teenager has suddenly become the brains behind a highly functioning team of drug traffickers.

Something is not right, Antoine concludes. He cannot accept that a seasoned drug boss like Willie would instruct Frankie to go after an innocent kid and his friends. Too risky a move for no apparent gain.

"Willie says they *is* bangin'!" Frankie cries. He does his best to answer, but he doesn't hide his feeling that his orders should simply be followed without any questions. "We got a job to do. You all need to shut up and do what I say."

He shoots Antoine a look as if to say he needs some backup.

"If Willie says we got to roll on Marshall's crew," says Antoine, "then that's what we got to do." Antoine zips up his backpack, puts on his headphones, and walks off. The meeting is over as far as he is concerned.

Antoine leaves the meeting frustrated. Part of him wishes he had never joined this ragtag group. He has run out of patience for Frankie's management style. Every idea that Frankie comes up with adds more risk and brings on more work for Antoine. Last week, Frankie upset a supplier by refusing to pay on time. Why? Antoine had no idea, but he had to step in and plead with the supplier—which included a 5 percent extra payment—not to walk away. Then, Frankie unexpectedly gave everyone three days vacation and shut down the drug-selling operations. Antoine quickly sent word to nervous customers that the group did not pause their business because they were being watched by police.

On it went. Frankie acts, Antoine must deal with the consequences.

Today's conversation feels like yet another example of Frankie's incompetence. Where did Frankie come up with the idea of going after an innocent kid? How much time would it take to deal with *this* stupid move? Should I just quit? The questions bounce around Antoine's head during his walk, all the way until he lands comfortably on the leather chair in the rear of Uncle Albert's storefront church. Leaning back into the chair doesn't immediately clear up his troubles. But for a few minutes, he can quiet his mind. Albert's house of worship is where Antoine can always find balance. A chance to reset.

With each breath, Antoine settles into the large brown-leather recliner. He feels dizzy and the radiator is on full blast. It doesn't help that his warmest down jacket is zipped up to the neck. No matter. He has come to the church seeking reckoning and clarity. And, according to his uncle Albert, the church is exactly where he should come in such moments. *You can't run from the Lord inside here*, Uncle Albert will tell all his parishioners.

Peering into the front room, Antoine sees choir practice about to end. Three retired women have stumbled their way through various gospel standards. They are accompanied by a sorrowful guitar, played by a seventy-five-year-old, once well-known local blues musician. As the guitar wails, the women raise their hands to the sky. The musician grins, closes his eyes, and massages one high-pitched note in time with the voices.

Antoine closes his eyes as the quartet launches into "Oh, What a Savior." Despite his wish to forget about Frankie, the situation on the streets creeps back into his head. Planning an attack on Marshall Mariot will be risky. Not only will he need to consider his own personal safety and that of his crew, but there are the longer-term consequences of getting caught by the police that weigh on him. Most notably, a criminal record will jeopardize his chance of going to college and securing financial aid.

One decision is becoming clearer by the minute. Antoine knows he will need to direct the team—Frankie will almost certainly mess things up. Another decision also seems clear. Antoine must carry a weapon with him. Just in case.

———

This leaves the matter of notifying his uncle. As the musician and singers leave, Uncle Albert makes his way to the anteroom. He lights a cigarette, pours himself some grape soda, and sits across from Antoine.

"We got robbed," Antoine says. Each week Antoine has been revealing to his uncle more of the workings of Frankie's crew, including his own role. So far, Uncle Albert has listened patiently, without calling the police or threatening to remove Antoine.

"They came up on us," Antoine continues. "Ain't nobody was hurt. But we lost more than a grand. Maybe more. But that ain't really the point. We just out there and they gonna keep coming back for us. That's for sure. This ain't the last time."

"*Mm-hmm,*" his uncle agrees. "So what's that tell you?"

"I don't know. Can't run no business this way, I guess," Antoine says, smirking. "But I think there's some other shit going on. Frankie just ain't keeping shit together. This ain't how I planned it, Uncle Albert. Wasn't supposed to be like this . . ."

Uncle Albert laughs. "Plans! Ah yes! Let me see. You feel that life ain't what you planned. Now tell that to God and see what his response gonna be. Real question, Antoine, is what *you* gonna do. Hell with plans. And the hell with Frankie! It ain't about him. You control yourself. That's all you can do."

"I'm doing this to help Momma, so fuck it, I'm going with it. But that nigger gonna get us killed."

"Ain't about him, Antoine. It's about *you.* I'll tell you why." Albert pops some M&M's in his mouth and gulps the rest of his soda. "You see, Antoine, this time it's that dumbass nigger. Next time it's some dumbass white man who's your boss. After that, it's your wife. You understand?"

Antoine shrugs. He's not in the mood for a sermon. All he wants is for his uncle to give him instructions.

"You need to ask yourself, what are you feeling about things? What can *you* do to control shit?"

Albert pauses. He can tell that Antoine is probably giving him only half the story. "You got something planned. I can tell, Antoine. So you just make sure that what you gonna do doesn't bring on new problems. See, that's what people don't always catch. You rush to solve this motherfucking problem and then you got ten more crawling up your ass. You understand?"

Antoine is quiet. Right or wrong, and as risky as it might be, he must find a way to make things work with Frankie's crew.

4

A faded, clover-green placard, with the five words

WELCOME TO THE O'MALLEY HOME

has hovered over the front door of Marshall Mariot's family home for forty years. Marshall's grandma let the sign remain in place when she purchased the property from an Irish family. She transferred the property to her son and daughter-in-law when her husband passed—but she insisted that the sign remain. She wanted Marshall's parents, Jay and Joycie, to appreciate this symbol of Chicago's Black freedom. Pioneers like her courageously purchased homes in Rosewood and other segregated white Chicago communities where Blacks were once excluded. Hers wasn't the first Black family to enter the Irish neighborhood, but her neighbors sure made her feel like they were.

That damn sign is the most important piece of wood on this whole house, Grandma liked to say at the dinner table. For good measure, she threw in a prayer for the souls of the deceased O'Malley clan.

Rosewood and the broader Chicago South Side is a sprawling American patchwork. Well-manicured homes break up the rolling weave of decaying bungalows and drab apartment buildings. The nearby steel mills no long color the air, but a heaviness and gray remains. Names on local signage—PULASKI, VALUKAS, ROSENTOWSKI—harkens back to a gritty past when Europe's aspiring migrants swallowed up the region. This was once blue-collar country—deeply racist, proud, and defiant, and defining what mid-century America would say of itself. Theirs was the bungalow, the parish church, and the corner bar. Theirs was white or black. Nothing in between.

White ethnic families have long gone. Civil rights victories propelled Black families like the Mariots—aching to flee overcrowded, blighted ghettos—southward from the central city into outlying neighborhoods. They looked for any available housing in Rosewood and beyond. Rabid real estate brokers nicely moved things along by spreading alarming stories of an incoming Black surge. The whites quickly turned and ran. Jay's father, a sanitation truck driver, and his mother, a county nurse, pooled their savings and quickly made an offer on the O'Malley home. Weathering racist graffiti on their car and bottles cast through the windows, they stayed put and hoped for a better day.

The seventies and eighties offered no hero's welcome to the Black families who followed in their path. Employment options withered in Chicago as large manufacturing firms relocated their plants overseas. Bitter poverty and hardship, and eventually drugs, took root on the South Side. Marshall's grandparents saved enough to retire. But others were not so lucky. The Mariots watched neighbor after neighbor picked off, one by one, by job loss, addiction, depression, and the unforgiving stigma of being on welfare. They watched as two and three sets of families crammed into units meant for one. Violence and a vibrant gang-controlled economy blossomed. Rosewood was well on the way to becoming another dense, segregated Chicago ghetto community.

Amidst all these changes, Marshall's grandparents raised four children in the house. Each completed high school and moved into their own home in a nearby working-class district. Marshall's father, Jay, was the youngest. He met Joycie at a local restaurant where she was waiting tables. The two married, and Joycie gave birth to three children, Marshall being the middle child.

Jay's job as a technician in a tool shop and Joycie's work as a caregiver also give the Mariots a necessary routine and predictability. The rules for the children are clear: no one may live in the house without being in school, working, or seeking employment. Homework is a priority, as is church on Sundays.

Neither Jay nor Joycie believes that school or work, by itself, is a guaranteed shield from the temptations of the streets. Jay has always been employed, but even he joined a gang as a teenager. He ended up in a knife fight, went off to prison for a short stint, and felt the stigma of dropping out of school. With the help of uncles, pastors, former schoolteachers, and a network of local adults, he straightened himself out, obtained his GED, and reentered the workforce. He has stayed out of trouble ever since.

Ordinary never got no one in trouble. This is Marshall's parents' favorite aphorism. If ever a sign were to replace the green placard that currently greets visitors to the Mariot bungalow, it would be that. Raising an *ordinary* young man in Rosewood is no small achievement for parents. Jay and Joycie discovered the word at a church sermon. It has become a convenient way for them to set expectations for all three children who duck and weave local hazards. *Go to school, have fun, come home, get a job if you can. Be ordinary.*

———

On Monday afternoons, Jay and Joycie will usually spend some time resting and making plans for the week ahead. The kids are usually at school and the house is quiet enough to talk. But today is different. Marshall storms into the house with his friend Georgie, saying hardly a word to them. The teens quickly barricade themselves in Marshall's bedroom.

Jay lies silently on the long leather couch, seeming not to pay much attention to the hubbub. Joycie, by contrast, walks up and down the living room, her arms folded across her chest. Every few minutes, she peers into the hallway and strains to decipher the hushed talk behind Marshall's bedroom door.

"You keep watching that door expecting someone to come out and deliver the news," Jay says just loud enough for Joycie to hear. "Sometimes it's best not to know."

"Marshall ain't right," Joycie whispers. She looks at the plate of food she prepared for her son—a ham sandwich, chips, and a slice of peach cobbler. A pretty rose-flowered tablecloth underneath.

On any other day, Joycie would have barged through the door to demand an explanation from her son. He was not working, skipping school, and avoiding her questions. *What's stopping me?* she wonders, knowing that she was not enforcing the rules that she and Jay had put in place for her kids. She confided to Jay that she had lost some confidence in the last few weeks. She worried her questioning was pushing Marshall even further away from her. She worried that if she took action—grounding him, preventing him from seeing his friends—he would get himself in more trouble out of spite. *Everything will just pass, just be patient,* the other moms on the block tell her. Too many voices in her head. She is confused and second-guessing her judgment.

"Best not to worry until you have something to worry about," Jay remarks, staying focused on the TV. He hopes Joycie will sit down. She could use the rest after spending all day at various jobs that keep her on her feet—nursing, cleaning, handling customers at a salon.

"That's the time when you'll have *plenty* to worry about," Joycie says with a grimace. She stands above Jay and stares him down. She needs her husband to give her some confidence by becoming a more active partner. "Ain't you gonna *do* something? Don't you want to know what's bothering your son?"

Jay does not answer. They have had the same conversation every night for two weeks. He shares her concern for Marshall. He has noticed the change in his son's mood. He tells Joycie he has *already* done everything a father can do. Talking, walking together, eating dinner at McDonald's. Jay's view is clear. If Marshall wishes to stay silent, it is his right as a man.

Last night, in a rare moment of excitement, Jay preached to his wife.

"Our son has to defend himself. Mom and Dad ain't gonna be

around forever to come to his rescue," he told Joycie. "I went through this, and if you just give him a little time—let him work it out by himself, he'll come back to us."

Jay knows Marshall is haunted. He knows because he too was haunted as a teen. He knows what it means to be a Black teen in Chicago, growing up on the streets. His son must learn to fight his battles, Jay reasons, thinking about his own battle as a teenager.

"I ain't saying what I did was the right thing, but it taught me to be a man."

Joycie has heard this speech before. Jay was a frustrated teen. He couldn't resist the lure of drug money. A knife fight became a shooting, which brought him prison time. "I had to learn the hard way. When I was in that cell, I had time to think. I ain't saying Marshall needs to go to prison, but maybe that bedroom is where he is thinking. And *I think* we should let him figure some things out by himself."

Jay keeps talking, but Joycie's mind drifts. She understands Jay's approach. Best a father can do is listen and stay within shouting distance. But, hers differs. Her own experience is based on early and active intervention. She prefers to come to the aid of her children before a terrible influence or influencer has time to settle. For their oldest child, this meant their confronting a twenty-two-year-old boy who wanted to date the fourteen-year-old Ophelia. *That boy is nearly twice your age and ready to be a daddy, which means you ain't ready for him!* After sharing this decision with Ophelia, she marched over to the boy's house and gave the parents a choice: either he stay away or she would register him with the police as a sexual predator.

For Marshall's sister Lanea the threat was a teenage friend who dangled the prospect of income as a gang lookout. Joycie came up with a six-month curfew—in the house by 6:00 p.m.—and told Lanea that she would be serving as a house cleaner with Aunt May on the weekends. A brilliant move, it turned out. Lanea became the source of envy among her school friends. She was now the one with money in her pocket. Her friends started looking for legit employment themselves. Lanea has been employed ever since and she is an above-average student.

Next up is Marshall. Crisis hasn't hit yet. No cops have visited, no calls from the prison or the hospital, and Joycie hasn't found any drug paraphernalia in his bedroom. Still, she can tell that her son is teetering. Her challenge is to winnow down the likely candidates of *bad shit* that is affecting her son—gangs, drugs, shoplifting. Her clues—refusal to eat, irritability, baggy eyes, late nights with friends—are thin. This is the behavior of most "normal" neighborhood teens.

On the other side of the bedroom door, Marshall and Georgie strategize. The bedroom became their war room when Marshall unexpectedly shared his fear of Frankie Paul. He revealed his shame at being unable to defend himself. And he vowed to do whatever it took to end his embarrassment and suffering. Marshall thought Georgie would be surprised to hear his news, but instead he laughed in solidarity.

"You ain't alone," Georgie shook his head. "*Everyone* is tired of those niggers. We got your back, Marshall. Don't worry."

Georgie talked about the incidents that never reached Marshall's ears. Like the afternoon when Frankie's crew badgered one of their friends in the park. Or the time Frankie spat at Georgie at an ice cream parlor. Or the weekend when some of Frankie's crew took Georgie's cash at the movie theater. One insult and public humiliation after another. Until then, Marshall's friends had remained mostly silent, suffering in quiet shame.

Marshall and his friends were athletes, video game players, and mountain bike riders. They spent hours gossiping on Facebook and Twitter and watching professional wrestling and horror movies on TV. They were not fighters or gangbangers or drug dealers. Their tolerance for risk was to sneak out at night for a cigarette and some beer, or to the malls on Chicago's Magnificent Mile where they could tease the packs of teenage girls who rode the train from Winnetka, Joliet, and Blue Island. None of them had been in a fistfight. No one had any experience with guns.

Over weeks of meetings on the stoop of the brownstone where Marshall's grandpa once lived, a common theme emerged. Everyone wanted to recover their dignity. Their honor was at stake, and they were having trouble holding their heads high in Rosewood. In all the social media channels, local kids talked about them as weak and scared. In private Facebook groups, girls called them "pussies." At weekend parties and in the school hallway, the talk was much the same—*Look at the little bitches!*

And, worst of all, the five teens knew they were hearing only a small part of local gossip and innuendo.

A consensus quickly emerged. We have to stop Frankie, they concluded. At any cost.

Jonny's presence at the meeting changed the mood of the group.

Until this point, Marshall never considered carrying a weapon. But he now sees some of the benefits of being armed when they confront Frankie. Perhaps they will look more intimidating. A gun could help them make the point that his friend Siron made on the stoop after Jonny brought out his large .44 caliber handgun—*When we roll up on that nigger with what Jonny offering, he ain't never gonna think about us again.*

After a long period of silence, Marshall whispers to Georgie. "I'll do it if you want."

"Good!" Georgie cries out with both relief and joy. "That's gonna make everyone else feel better. Ain't like we got to use it or nothing. Just that maybe we should carry it."

"Only problem is, how we gonna *get it*?" asks Marshall.

"From Jonny," Georgie responds, confused about the question. "Who else?!"

"Damn! I ain't got that kind of money!" Marshall shakes his head at the thought of paying several thousand dollars for Jonny's beautiful black gun.

"He's got other ones," Georgie says. "That's what he does."

"Why can't he just give us one for the night? We could pay him?" Marshall asks.

"Don't think it works like that." Georgie shrugs.

"How does it work then?! If we ain't gonna use it, why we need to buy it?" Marshall wants to know.

"Man, let's just get one, okay? Anyway, if you think about it, Frankie is gonna keep coming back at us, right? So, we probably need to have one around."

"Okay, but where we keeping it?" Marshall asks.

"Right here," Georgie says.

"No way!" Marshall yells. He can only imagine what his father will do if he finds a weapon in his room.

And yet Marshall knows Dad will also be proud. *My son is taking care of his shit!* Marshall imagines Dad saying to the family. Mom and Dad always tell him to act like a grown up. Even Grandma has gotten into the act—*Me and Grandpa were out working full-time when we turned sixteen!* She reminds him of this nearly every morning before school. But, with her health failing, she has been a less forceful presence in the house.

Grandpa would want me to take control, Marshall thinks. *Grandpa would want me to take care of my shit.*

"We got to get going. Let's go and see Jonny," Marshall cries out, jumping off the bed.

Marshall and Georgie burst through the bedroom door and into the living room. Georgie rushes past Marshall's parents without offering as much as a nod of his head.

"Going to stay over Georgie's house tonight, Momma!" Marshall shouts. "Already told Dad about it. I love you, Momma, you know that, don't you?"

Joycie doesn't say a word. She takes in her son's face. Marshall's cheeks are flush and his eyes have receded into their sockets. He looks possessed. Joycie holds back tears.

"You know I love you, right?!" Marshall asks hurriedly.

Joycie nods as tears stream down her face. Marshall turns toward the door. He cannot look at his father.

The screen door slams behind Marshall and Joycie drops onto the couch next to her husband. Instinctively, she grabs Jay's cool, sweaty hands. He too is shaking. Dad also knows that their son is not right.

5

Thursday morning, the alarm on Frankie's phone rings, waking him up from a fitful night of sleep. He has an hour before his meeting with Antoine. He scans his phone for a message from Calvin. Nothing.

Son of a bitch lied to me, Frankie mutters to himself.

Calvin promised to find him a new handgun—one that could replace the pistol he has been carrying around for the last few months. Frankie said he found the gun in Willie's basement, which concerned Calvin. It was old and unreliable—and probably had other crimes on it, which cops could trace back to Willie. Best to find a new weapon for Frankie, Calvin reasoned. Frankie was sure that Calvin would come through, especially after he told him in confidence that he would be planning a surprise attack on a neighboring gang. Frankie felt Calvin would surely understand his motives: not only does he need a reliable weapon for the attack, but his crew has to look tough to deter others who may be planning a takeover.

"Don't say nothing to Willie," Frankie told Calvin. "He's gonna like it when it all goes down. I'm taking out some niggers that's been messing with us. But you gotta get me some protection."

"You taking charge. I like that. And Willie has been looking for that in you. So do what you need to." Calvin's response was inspirational. Frankie felt like his decision to attack Marshall was the right one. But Calvin also cautioned Frankie against doing something that would bring about increased police attention, like firing his weapon instead of just waving it around for show.

"Just scare the bitch and then move on. Don't get greedy, Frankie." Calvin warned, encouraging Frankie not to become too ambitious with his intended show of strength.

Calvin said he would do his best to deliver a new weapon in twenty-four hours. But Frankie has heard nothing from the prison guard since their meeting, He is losing hope that Calvin will come through. *Fuck it*, he thinks to himself. *I'm still gonna carry.* Frankie decides to bring the old gun on the attack, even if risky to do so.

Frankie reaches next to his bed and grabs a Chicago Bulls jersey—Scottie Pippen #33. It is one of fifty Chicago sports team shirts that sit in a large pile, alongside another two-foot-high collection of vintage Nike sneakers. His five-by-five-foot basement corner, with a fraying, dingy mattress and sleeping bag, is what he has been calling a bedroom since Willie rescued him from foster care. He never complained about sleeping in an unheated, poorly ventilated basement, in a house crowded with eight other family members leaning on Willie's kindness for a place to live. He didn't care about the mice that left droppings on his mattress or the roaches that climbed the walls. He pays fifty dollars per month rent and goes about his business.

Frankie gulps the remains of last night's Mountain Dew, throws on some jeans, and sends one more text to Calvin—Fuck! I need 2 know. U got it?—before running out the door to meet Antoine.

———

Frankie pulls up to Samir's bodega, a small convenience store across the street from Holden Park, and a few blocks from the house where his team traffics drugs. Antoine is working on the day's schedule, assigning people shifts and figuring out if they have enough supplies to stay open through the evening. Rain clouds hover overhead. Frankie steps through a lot strewn with garbage, which has become a feeding ground for a band of pigeons. The two leaders grab two empty milk crates and sit down to finish some donuts and sodas before settling into their meeting.

The night before, around six o'clock, Frankie called Antoine with his decision to go after Marshall right away.

"We need to hit them boys this weekend," he told his lieutenant. Frankie knew he needed to act fast. He had heard a rumor from his friend Tulia that his rival, Mo-Mo, planned to come after him. He trusted the intel since Tulia was dating the head of security for Mo-Mo. This was all he needed to hear to call Antoine with his decision.

Antoine was up most of the night, talking and texting with teammates to alert everyone that the plans were being sped up. This only brought about more questions and uncertainties. Everyone pestered him with the same questions—*Is it too late to change the plan? Is the attack really necessary? Are we ready? What will happen if they just refuse to join?*

"Everything is set," Antoine says, without looking at Frankie. The activity from last night has left him groggy and he is in a sour mood. He usually spends his Thursdays at his mother's side. But not today. With a raid upcoming, Antoine knows he needs to focus his energy on preparing the inexperienced group for what lies ahead. "I told everyone we gonna make our move right away."

Antoine then tells Frankie that he has some information about Marshall's crew—the result of paying two homeless men twenty dollars each to snoop around the neighborhood. "They ain't bang-ing, they ain't selling no dope," Antoine starts off. "And they prob-ably ain't holding more than a few Glocks—or maybe something smaller." Frankie is impressed with the level of detail that two homeless men could gather in such a short period of time. He re-minds himself to ask Antoine how he consistently is able to obtain such detailed intel on their enemies.

"They're young, so we got to be careful. They could be trying to prove themselves out there. They use that old building across the way, past that little lake right by where niggers be running ball in the morning."

Antoine pauses, as if reviewing some notes in his head, then makes a recommendation. "I'm guessing you want to drive and do something quick, but we could walk up on them," Antoine says. "Might be better. No 5-0. We just get there and do our thing. Easy."

"No, no, no," Frankie says, shaking his head and frustrated that Antoine still doesn't agree with his preference to carry out a drive-by raid. Frankie wants the symbolism of pulling up in a car and making a big show. "We *got* to drive. They gonna look at us like we serious, Antoine."

Antoine tries again to point out the problems with driving. "Cops gonna hear us, people gonna see us—"

"Fuck it! We got to make it so they don't mess with us no more," Frankie says.

Antoine is silent. Thirty seconds pass. One minute. No response.

Antoine has spent the past many hours looking into the ways to confront Marshall's group. Like so many of Frankie's unexpected moves, this one also forces upon Antoine a risk-reward calculation. A drive-by looks simple—everyone gets in the car, heads over for a beating, and then leaves. And there is one potential benefit for Antoine: in the car, he can manage the group, and reduce the likelihood that they might do something foolish.

But nothing is so simple when it comes to his team, which is new to street conflict. Antoine knows fear is his greatest obstacle to any planned drive-by attack. Even if his team is initially enthusiastic, over time some will want to walk away. He will need to convince them to join, whether with money or a promise of a beatdown if they refuse. There are also practical challenges—finding a car, tracing the route, addressing any risks along the way. All of this work will fall on him.

For all these reasons, Antoine would prefer a different tactic: one afternoon, the crew ends their drug sales early, runs over to Marshall's hangout, taunts the group with whatever threats Frankie feels is necessary, gets into a fistfight if necessary, and then runs home. This feels less risky, with fewer unforeseen consequences. And, if the police come after them, the response will always be more lenient than if they attacked by car—which cops look at as more serious and threatening.

Frankie finally asks him, "So, what you think? You understand what I'm saying?"

"Okay, we drive," Antoine says, giving in. He decides he needs control over the group. And he will be driving, so he can always call things off if shit doesn't feel right.

Frankie nods, gets up, and starts talking about how the drive-by will go down. "We gonna roll up on these niggers!" Antoine quickly shoots him a glare—a "shut the fuck up!" order. Noticing that his exuberance has attracted the attention of the small crowd outside Samir's, Frankie quiets his voice and takes a seat on the crate. He continues his narration with a hard whisper in Antoine's ear.

In the distance, Antoine spots the other team members running over to them, weaving in and out of cars. He empties the last of two large bottles of Mountain Dew on the ground. Frankie casts aside a remaining donut wrapper and throws up a few gang signs as the boys near.

———

By noon, everyone is assembled inside a rusty Ford Fairlane. Antoine has paid a friend $500 to loan his car for the attack—this is not a sum of money a local youth can easily turn away. Antoine wants the group to become familiar with the drive over to Marshall's hangout. Today will be a practice run and a chance for him to finish sketching out the plans for their ambush.

The car idles next to a bruised trash can at the eastern end of Holden Park—a short walk from the brownstone where Marshall's friends gather. A distressed sign with peeling rust and graffiti sits head high and stares down at Frankie and the others in the car. WELCOME TO HOLDEN PARK — KEEP YOUR SHIT TO YOURSELF! Underneath, there is a pile of empty beer bottles, a few empty packs of cigarettes, and a torn copy of a local newspaper.

Frankie looks over at Antoine, who appears to be asleep while holding the steering wheel. If it was anyone else, Frankie would say something. But Antoine is the only one in the car whose judgment he trusts. Frankie knows Antoine is the only one capable of directing their plans.

Frankie peers at the back seat to check out his crew. *If only Willie could see me now!* He can see the smile on his cousin's face when Calvin, their emissary, files his report: *Frankie took down that enemy, just like you wanted, Willie.*

All Frankie wants is Willie's approval. That and avoiding another stint in foster care. He knows Willie will be pissed that he went after a group of kids who were never really a threat. But *fuck it!* Frankie keeps telling himself. After they beat the crap out of Marshall and his friends, the crew is sure to look tougher on the streets. Like they went after an *enemy*.

Frankie nudges Antoine awake and then glances back at the three members of his team. Cramped in the back seat, they are texting and peeking at one another's Facebook feeds. He hopes they are following instructions and not posting about the raid. No one seems particularly animated by the fact they are warming up for their first group assault.

What would Willie do to get everyone on edge? Frankie wonders, channeling his cousin, who is several hundred miles away in a cold prison cell. He considers berating the group but recalls

Willie's reminder to motivate his team with positive sentiments. "Tell 'em they gonna make that cash, people gonna respect them for being motherfucking killers!" Willie told him several times before heading to prison. He then recalls that Antoine is directing today's team meeting. If his lieutenant doesn't mind the inattentiveness, so be it.

Antoine places the car in gear and pulls out for the practice run. He barks out instructions to the others. "Don't look at anyone, don't yell out the window, turn your phones off, don't take no pictures."

Frankie nudges Antoine and whispers, "The *other* thing. You keep forgetting to tell them about the *other thing*."

Antoine nods and pulls over the car. "You tell them," he instructs Frankie.

Frankie pulls back his hood and does his best to sound managerial.

"Can't take nothing off these boys, you got that? Not sure why—" Frankie pauses and looks over at Antoine. He is confused. He casts his second-in-command a glance, as if to ask, *Why is it that we can't rob anyone of money or jewelry during the beatdown?*

Antoine takes over. He looks back at everyone in the rearview mirror. "All we doing is telling them boys not to fuck with us. That's it. So, no guns. And no *taking no shit off nobody*. I know you want to go after their money, but don't! This turns into a robbery and cops will come down on you real bad. If it's a beatdown, it's 'he said, she said' shit. Dig?"

Everyone looks nervous. And confused. The intricacies of drive-by protocol are lost on them. There are too many rules to remember. Their heads bob up and down approvingly but they are lost.

"I know you can do this." Antoine turns around and smiles. He can sense the team's uncertainty. They need encouragement. "We gonna get these niggers, right?"

Meek smiles and shaky grins appear from the back seat. Then some tepid handshakes. Antoine turns around and starts punching everyone spiritedly. The roughhousing is helping. The car begins to sway like a boat and Frankie shouts, "Let's get them niggers!" Antoine puts the car back in gear and pulls away just as droppings from a bird splatter onto the windshield, obstructing his view.

6

Marshall's sister Lanea grabs her backpack and a chocolate muffin from the kitchen table and sprints out of the back door. She does not want to linger—fearing her mother will pepper her with questions about Marshall, who has been acting strangely. She sends Marshall a two-character text—5! She will meet him in five minutes at the brownstone stoop.

She empathizes with Marshall. She hears the rumors being circulated about her brother and his friends, and she spoke earlier with Georgie about the group's plans. She cringes when others call him a pussy and she actively defends him on social media. But her patience is wearing thin. Marshall is isolating himself from everyone who could help him. She wants him to speak with their father, but she knows this is not likely to happen—and, even if they talk, Marshall will not disclose what is really going on.

For the moment, she decides that her best option is to listen to Marshall and offer advice. Marshall has always trusted her. They have always been close. Though she was his junior, she was also a caretaker. She always knew when Marshall was bothered. She always approached with an empathetic ear and a helping hand. In fact, a week ago, she mentioned taking notice of Marshall's failing mood. She had some ideas that he should consider. Last night, he finally reached out to her. "I need to talk with you about something after breakfast tomorrow." They agreed to meet at the brownstone.

———————

Lanea walks down the street toward him. Marshall wants to reveal *everything* to her. But can he muster up the courage to be candid? A part of him believes that transparency should not be difficult. After all, he has been revealing his secrets to Lanea since they were toddlers. It was at an early age that Lanea took hold of the word "psychologist." She made it her passion. While other children went after toys, she went after secrets. She practiced on her family. Dad told her about his prison time. Momma revealed her financial anxieties. And Grandma even told her that she felt the Lord might abandon her at times. Lanea listened and offered advice. Not bad for an eight-year-old.

Marshall was part of her case load. He told her about all his pranks, sometimes making things up so Lanea would have more stories to work with. They have spent a decade playing therapist-patient with one another.

Lanea runs over toward the stoop, sprints up the steps, and plops down next to him. Before she can settle, Marshall launches into his confession. Everything comes out in one long sentence. The feud with Frankie, the plan to confront him, his fears. All of it.

Lanea starts to laugh. "Damn, slow down," she says, opening

up her black North Face jacket. "I already know about what you telling me! You think Georgie and I don't talk or something?"

Marshall is surprised to hear that his best friend, Georgie, has been communicating with his sister. He leaves that tidbit alone. There's too much else to worry about.

"And I know what you're *about* to do," she says. "I ain't gonna stop you because *Frankie* ain't gonna stop fucking with you."

Marshall is now stunned. How does Lanea know anyone in Frankie Paul's crew?! Before he can ask, Lanea explains.

"I found out something from Booty, who runs with Frankie. He runs with that girl I know, Cindy. He told her everything. He said they would be coming after you. Frankie thinks you want to take over his thing—you know, his business. So they gonna stop you."

The surprises just keep coming for Marshall. He has no idea how Frankie came to view him as a drug dealer, much less a competitor who is after his business. He puts the pieces together: Frankie is dealing dope. He believes Marshall is running a gang on the other side of Holden Park. He wants to take Marshall down before Marshall tries to capture his sales spot. Makes sense, except for the fact it's all wrong.

Before pointing out the obvious errors to his sister, Marshall pauses. He finds an unexpected pleasure in Frankie's assessment that he is capable of directing organized crime. Outside of his grandparents, no one ever saw that much potential in him.

"Want to know what you should do?" Lanea asks. "You need to tell Dad. I know you think I'm crazy, but he can help you. I don't see you as no fighter, Marshall. And, these niggers gonna come after you and, they gonna be shooting. They ain't gonna talk to you or nothing. Just gonna shoot you. Is that what you want?"

"I'm ready for them," Marshall stands up and shouts. He points his finger into the air like a gun. "I'm gonna be ready, Lanea! And I'll shoot back. I will."

It is at that moment that Lanea recognizes where things stand. She knows what every young person in Rosewood understands at a deep level: Peer pressure changes everything. Marshall is no longer the innocent kid bullied on the playground. Things have grown worse than she imagined. She knows Marshall would not decide by himself to confront Frankie. Nor would he come up with the idea of carrying a gun. This must have been a group decision. Consequently, for Marshall to back off suddenly and walk away will mean losing face with his friends—which is even harsher than a public shaming at the hands of Frankie Paul.

She quickly reconsiders her own options in light of this new information. Yes, Dad can still help, but she will need something more than a caring sibling plea to convince Marshall to call upon their father. Should she tell Dad herself? Doing so can get Marshall out of trouble short term, but it could damage his reputation locally. He will be viewed as weak and fearful. A nobody. And he will end up alone like a fish out of the fishbowl lunging about helplessly. On top of this, Marshall may lose trust in his sister for breaking confidences and speaking with their father.

Lanea decides that there is no point trying to undo what's been done. The best she can do is to help Marshall fight back. Her focus must be to make the eventual altercation with Frankie less likely to cause harm.

"If you go after that nigger, don't bring no gun with you," she says. "Just do it and get it over with. He won't mess with you no more."

Marshall stares off into the distance.

"I'm serious, Marshall. All you need to do is show that boy you can't be messed with!" Lanea's voice rises sharply in an attempt to get Marshall's attention. Seeing that he is not going to answer, she gives up. "Momma making fish for Grandma's birthday. Don't be late."

"Can't. Got to meet with Georgie tonight," Marshall says, grabbing his backpack. He races off, leaving Lanea alone with her thoughts and fears.

Marshall is in too deep. Lanea narrows her potential actions to three: She can do nothing. She can approach her dad. Or she can go directly to the heart of the problem—a meetup with Frankie Paul. She vows to make up her mind by the end of the day.

7

The practice run is over. Antoine leans against the window of the Noodle King. The fast-food restaurant is hopping as workers straggle in from the meat supply store across the street. Antoine sips on a soda and eats his lunch—lo mein with pork.

He takes stock of the practice run. His team is as green as Marshall's crew. They have no experience with street fighting and firearms. And the team leader, Frankie, is barely competent.

He tried to keep the plan for an evening ambush on Marshall simple and easy for his team to follow. He told everyone he would be the driver for their passage down Stony Island Avenue and across the park to Marshall's brownstone. He assigned everyone a simple task along the drive—Frankie will look out for cops, Booty will look out for suspicious groups of people, Tiny will see if any known enemy gang members were around. The car will first take cover behind the large, rusty dumpster adjacent to the basketball court. Booty will sneak out the back and remove the car's license plates. Then, on their first pass by the brownstone, everyone but

Antoine will jump out and execute the beatdown. Antoine will drive off and spin around to pick them up. They will exit via the alley behind Samir's store. No guns, no robbery, just a little show of force.

On the practice run, Antoine noticed one problem. Only one route to speed away. If cops are nearby, they will be stuck without a safe exit.

Antoine also identified hazards coming from his own team. Highest on the list is the fact that no one listens carefully. People forgot their assigned duties, some were checking social media — which concerned Antoine since he asked them not to communicate their plans to anyone outside the group.

It is the conversation with his cousin, Blake, that is fresh on his mind after the practice run. Blake, an ex-gang member, turned his own life around after a prison sentence for drug trafficking. Antoine shared some of his challenge with Blake yesterday.

"I'm going to drive these boys over for a beatdown," he told Blake. "Should I carry or not?"

Blake weighed the options — if they were caught, being armed would piss off the cops, who might look the other way for a street fight but come down hard for an armed battle.

"I'm thinking you ain't got no choice, Antoine," Blake said directly. "Frankie can't run shit and he'll get you in trouble if you don't watch out."

"Yeah, maybe I'll take a gun, but not use it," Antoine said.

That prompted another reflection and response by Blake. "Here's what I learned in prison. Halfway is half-ass. Never start gangbangin' half-ass. If you deciding to run Frankie's team, then *do the thing*! Take it over. Otherwise, get the fuck out. Smart, young niggers land in County lockup 'cause they couldn't decide who they is. Do it or get the fuck out. *Now*."

Antoine knows Blake is right. He needs to stop hesitating— stop thinking of Frankie's team as a way station. Go all in or get out. Taking his cousin Blake's advice, he immediately sent a text to a friend, Missie Bateson, who sells guns in Rosewood. The first one read Got to get with you, now!

Missie responded. IGU-24. (I will get back to you in twenty-four hours). But Antoine was impatient, so he sent another. Yo! I got to have what you got. Where you at?

This prompted another, more comforting response. Slo, Coming2U (Be patient, I'm on it). Missie is an experienced gun seller whom Antoine can trust. Not only will she help him find a weapon but she will probably share intel on Marshall. And, as someone experienced with local conflict, she will advise him on whether being armed is an appropriate move for the young lieutenant.

8

Marshall leaves Lanea, stops at Samir's bodega to grab a grape soda, and races over to the brownstone. His friends have been waiting for him. No one is interested in attending school. For the last few days, they have been skipping class, leaving school early, and hanging out together. They know they need to stick together to plan their revenge on Frankie.

Marshall runs up the stairs, and out of breath, cries out what he has learned from his sister. "Frankie thinks we're coming after him. We got to think about whether we want to creep on him. He may come out shooting."

His friends express no alarm, which surprises Marshall. He expected to see fear, hesitation, and a reluctance to follow through with their plan. Instead, Georgie, Siron, and the others show resolve. They shout at one another.

"I ain't afraid."

"I say we go after him tonight!"

"When is Jonny bringing us the gun? Let's go as soon as we get it."

Handshakes and fist pumps follow. Siron holds his phone up, using it as a speaker to play a song from a local rapper.

Marshall does not want to dampen their enthusiasm. This is what he has always wanted—friends who are committed to defending him. *But is it* really *safe to go down this road*, he wonders.

Marshall softly reminds them who they are up against. "Lanea told me a few other things. Frankie's got a cousin in prison. It's Willie—the one who they say shot them two people in Calumet. And Willie's the one who *really* runs the shit. I sure as hell don't want him coming after us!"

Georgie shakes his head and takes out a half-eaten sandwich from his pocket. He takes a bite and shouts at the group. "Willie ain't thinking about us! Hell no. Probably doesn't even know what's going on. Let's figure out when we're going over there. I'm ready!"

Siron chimes in, also minimizing Marshall's concern. "I say we hit those niggers when they're alone. I know where they all hang out. Right over there, where that streetlight is. He selling dope 24-7. We can jump on them and—"

"Hold on!" Marshall interrupts. "I thought we was just sending a message to Frankie."

"Yeah! We *are* sending a message!" Siron yells. "We take care of some of his boys. Then he'll listen and leave us alone."

Everyone starts posing for selfies as though they've just won a tournament. Each pulls out a phone. They talk about the posts they will send out on their Instagram and Facebook feeds after a successful attack. They need their peers in Rosewood to know they're not taking any more of Frankie's shit.

"I say we take all their dope and sell it ourselves!" Siron yells. "Maybe they got guns. We should get them too."

"*Oooh!* Yes! And let's sell their guns back to Jonny!"

Georgie refocuses their attention. "When we gonna do this?! Let's figure this shit out. When is Jonny bringing us the gun? Siron?"

Siron shrugs. "Ask Marshall. He probably knows."

Everyone looks at Marshall, who has lost command over the meeting.

"Don't know," Marshall says. He shakes his head and turns the other way. He wishes they would reconsider this plan to go after Frankie. He still wishes that they would simply walk up to Frankie, issue a warning, and then leave.

Siron suggests they head over to Frankie's turf next Tuesday. This is the day when welfare payments are issued and the pace of business picks up for Frankie's crew. The others agree that Frankie will not only be surprised by a Tuesday ambush, but that his team will be shamed in front of their customers.

Everyone is on board. Except for Marshall. Georgie nudges his friend. "Marshall, what do you think?"

"Don't know about this," Marshall mutters. He is sullen and frustrated at losing influence over the group. "I'm telling you, it don't feel right."

Lanea's voice from a few hours ago rumbles through his head. *You should talk with Dad. He can help.*

Georgie is impatient. Frustrated, he knows he must keep things moving forward. He watches Marshall climb down off the stoop and run across the street toward Samir's.

"Don't worry," Georgie says calmly to the others, though no one seems to be paying Marshall any mind. "Marshall is in. Let's just figure out what time we hitting Frankie!"

The group is animated. They shout out half-baked ideas.

"Let's take their shit and sell it!"

"I say we take over that spot. Kick 'em out. Man, I need to make some money too."

Georgie reminds them that they need to make a deposit with Jonny for the weapon. "You all got to bring me whatever you got at home. Nobody's holding back, right?" Georgie tells Siron to notify Jonny that they will have money for him by evening. "Probably, around two hundred dollars or two fifty is what I'm guessing."

Georgie and the group then decide they will go after Frankie's crew next Tuesday—five days from now. The group is one step closer to their goal of ending their suffering at the hands of Frankie Paul.

PART **2**

9

Waking up to the glare of a clear, bright autumn sky, Missie Bateson looks out of her third-floor apartment and sighs. She will celebrate an anniversary this month. For nearly a decade, she has sold outlawed goods in Rosewood. Guns, stolen car parts and credit cards, fake IDs and medical prescriptions. Never once has she been behind bars. A few close calls—two arrests, shot at a half dozen times, and robbed a half dozen more.

From her bedroom window, Missie stares at the line of office workers waiting to catch the commuter bus. A trail of Black folk, hunched over and weary, queue up to head downtown for various low-paying jobs—cleaner and clerk, bus driver and security guard. She sees the same set of workers, greeting the same bus driver, ignoring the same homeless couple begging for change.

This place is small. Too damn small, Missie thinks to herself. She shakes her head as she lights the first cigarette of the morning.

When a conflict brews in Rosewood, it is not only the aggrieved—like Frankie, Marshall, and their respective crews—whose lives are upended. Street fighting will wake up a wider cast of local characters. Such as those who work in the gun trade. People like Missie.

Marshall and Georgie are working with one type of local gun seller—Jonny Isaac. Hustlers like Jonny are always around. They can make a buck by selling firearms or finding a customer for another dealer. But they are amateur vendors, responsible for only a small percentage of local gun sales.

Missie works in a more stable side of the city's gun market—call it "professional" compared to Jonny's amateur dabbling. She is an accomplished *pro* whose family has been in the game for decades. Missie's father worked for rail transport firms in Illinois, Michigan, and Wisconsin for twenty years until an injury made it hard for him to leave home for extended periods. He retreated to his South Side Chicago bungalow, but he stayed in touch with farmers, small-town gun traders, gun store owners, and others with stocks of used weapons that could be sold to the gangs, criminals, and homeowners seeking protection back in Chicago. He served as the go-between until a customer attempted to rob him outside his home. Missie's father resisted and ran inside the house to find his weapons. He never made it inside the door—six shots in the back took his life.

Missie was the only one who could take over and became the primary income earner. Dad taught her well. She is now a trusted source for firearms in Rosewood. She supports her mother and seventeen-year-old sister and pays the rent on a three-bedroom flat near Holden Park.

As managers of family businesses, pro dealers are local creatures. Because the *same damn people shoot the same damn people for the same damn reasons*, as Missie will say when a new opportunity pops us, pros stay close and keep watch. Picking up the scent of a simmering dispute, even if it is just a bunch of teens, may lead to a potential client.

Today, cigarette in hand, she kicks off her Wednesday morning in her bathroom, brushing her teeth and staring intently at a second set of text messages.

Message #1:

Yo! I got to have what you got. Where you at?

Message #2:

3 CLEAN sticks. GL17. 2X, 2X, 2X. 48.

She compares the two. This first is secretive, but the intent is clear. It is from Antoine, Frankie Paul's lieutenant. Antoine is an old friend of the family. Missie grew up with Antoine. She knows he is under stress because of his mother's health, but something about the request does not ring true. The stress alone wouldn't motivate Antoine—who usually stays out of trouble—to purchase a weapon.

Thought Antoine was at college, Missie wonders. *Why does he need a gun? This ain't right.*

The second message is recognizable street code: *3 CLEAN sticks. GL17. 2X, 2X, 2X. 48.* (I want three handguns, Glock 9mms preferably, that have not been used in any previous crimes; I need them in two days and will pay two times the asking price.) The text is from Calvin the prison guard, Willie the incarcerated kingpin's emissary who communicates on his behalf. Calvin is a repeat customer of Missie's who buys guns for several local gangs.

Missie checks the time. She has thirty minutes to make the weekly meeting of her team—a Rosewood-based outfit that sells guns locally. She cannot be late. Her boss will start the meeting without her. She must finish making oatmeal for her mother, shower, and walk five blocks to Holden Park.

Missie's boss emphasizes preparation, especially when it comes to new customers. Missie knows she needs more information before she can present these two new requests. No time to shower. She needs to answer a few questions quickly—*What's the motive? Is there a gang war? Any red flags to be aware of?* She may have time for a few quick calls to sources—but she may also need to draw on her experience and make a few educated guesses about what's happening.

Missie stirs the oatmeal for her mother, who sits patiently in the living room. Her sister shouts "See you tonight!" and slams the door behind her as she heads off to class. Missie keeps thumbing her way past both morning text messages, hoping to divine some hidden insight. A nice commission awaits if she can pull off these two sales. A four-gun transaction will mean several hundred dollars in her pocket.

She looks again at Calvin's message. She knows that Calvin is a courier for five of Rosewood's drug dealing gangs. He will shuttle requests to her from gang leaders who are in prison or on the streets. But not every one of the five is a likely candidate. Four have already purchased large caches of firearms in the last three months. And they are not involved in a gang war. Missie rules them out.

This leaves Willie's crew. It's no secret that the kingpin's business is in trouble. Word on the street is that a takeover of Willie's territory is imminent. Missie's crew has been on the lookout for possible violence.

Missie considers the information at hand. She concludes that since Willie is in prison, there must be a new leader who has a problem. This is the likely person who will use the three weapons that Calvin wishes to purchase. A few more calls will let her know that the new leader is Frankie Paul.

Back to Message #1. The one from Antoine Wilson. Her childhood friend. Again, Missie asks herself, *Why does Antoine want a weapon?* She has no good answer.

Missie places the piping hot bowl of oatmeal in front of her mother, kisses her on the forehead, and then races out the front door with a diet Coke in hand. She lights her cigarette and heads down the street, toward the eastern entrance of Holden Park. Waiting for the traffic lights change, she sends out multiple texts to a few associates on the street who might provide her more information about Willie's crew. Her team will be waiting. Her boss will expect her timely arrival. *This place is too damn small.*

Missie looks up and notices another long line of office workers at the edge of the park, waiting for the #4 bus heading downtown. She stops and stares as the bus's brakes squeak sharply and the vehicle comes to a sudden stop. She sighs, imagining herself getting on. But, in her case, she would be heading in the other direction.

To breathe and find some relief, Missie will take a late afternoon bus ride southward, down one of the long avenues that stretches from downtown to the southern suburbs. The work takes its toll on Missie. Listening to the stories of the distressed and pissed-off is no easy task, and a long bus ride enables her to quiet the chatter in her mind. Stony Island Avenue, Cottage Grove Avenue. These are her favorite routes. Every few weeks, for a few bucks, she boards her Chicago Transit Authority bus and travels the stretch of Black neighborhoods that reach to the Indiana border. She'll get off, eat lunch at Steeltown Diner, and head back before her sister comes home from school. It gives her the chance to feel part of a bigger world—or at least see different street signs.

On occasion, the promise of escape is interrupted. A customer will recognize her on the bus, strike up a conversation, and inquire about a weapon. Or an urgent text will force her to return to Rosewood.

Wistfully staring at the bus, the opportunity in front of her— the potential sale to Calvin and another to Antoine—pops back into her head. Missie has a feeling something more is going on. She has a feeling these two fates—these two lives—are intertwined. Missie knows enough to trust her gut. Experience tells her *these two people have something to do with each other*.

10

"Harpoon." This is the nickname Jeremiah Harrison acquired as an eight-year-old. It happened quickly, twenty years ago. His uncle watched the young nephew sit attentively in the living room, listening to an older sister reading a story about hunting whales. Young Harrison pranced around the room, pretending to be a whaler. He shouted at his family, sixteen people living cramped in a two-story bungalow: "I'm gonna head out to the ocean and kill that whale!" Uncle Terrance laughed and applauded his nephew's determination. "You do that, Harpoon! And don't ever come back to this shithole!"

Harpoon. The name stuck. It is the street name of one of Chicago's most successful gun dealers—who is also Missie Bateson's boss.

Twenty *years* later, Harpoon is standing patiently in the northeast corner of Holden Park, waiting for Missie and the rest of the team to arrive. He warms his hand with a cup of tea. Nearby, four middle-aged men play pickup basketball while a band of homeless men rub their hands over a fire in a metal barrel. A merciless lake-shore wind swirls the leaves and shakes the branches in the surrounding oaks. The ducks head for cover under the bramble and tall grass shoots. Harpoon tears off pieces of dry white bread to bring them back.

Midweek is a slow time in the gun trade. Customers will not be thinking about their weekend needs for at least another twenty-four hours. This is perfect timing for a team meeting.

Harpoon has worked diligently to put together the right mix of talent. Sally looks out for cops. Juni hires local residents part-time for extra security. Lena is the wise money manager. Felicity launders cash by striking deals with local businesses. And Missie recruits all hired contractors and supervises out-of-town purchasing. Everyone is experienced at their craft.

There is one job that is shared by the entire team: handling customers. A request to purchase a weapon always presents risks. The customer may appear to be innocent—just another human seeking protection. But the crew must look out for undercover cops and moles from an enemy crew intent on stealing their cash and weapons. This creates an "all hands on deck" approach: one person will introduce a new potential customer, but everyone is responsible for vetting the inquiry.

At the end of September, Harpoon's team is busy recovering from the frenzied pace of the summer. Autumn gun sales are not colored by ever-present summer conflict. When September rolls around, the street rhythms settle. Tempers still flare, but across the neighborhood, children and families fall into patterns, with more of their lives indoors and apart from each other. The antagonisms will be distinct—like cliquish schoolyard fights that turn serious—and drawn-out gang fights that spread out over the course of an entire winter.

For Harpoon's team, autumn is a chance to reflect. They use the time to stock up on inventory, and to address personal and family matters that had to be ignored during the hot summer months. Invariably, this means a time to consider whether the risks of gun trading are worth the rewards.

Missie arrives to find a blanket filled with snacks—chips, homemade cobbler, pork rinds smothered in hot sauce. Lena's pregnancy is making them all hungrier than usual. It is not accidental that Harpoon has recruited local women in their twenties and thirties. He believes that, no matter how well trained, police never scrutinize women as closely as men. The ladies carry a low profile—what he calls maintaining a "plain Jane" attitude.

Harpoon begins today's meeting as he does every other—with the words of another of his uncles, Jake: *You make a sale, but you buy a relationship*. Just as Missie's father, Lawrence, trained her, Uncle Jake was one of several elders who mentored Harpoon in the ways of trafficking. There are always two dozen such elders on Chicago's South Side passing on their craft to sons and daughters, nieces and nephews. It is a club of friendly competitors, pros who have built a feeling of mutual respect for one another. Uncle Jake and Lawrence never collaborated—most of these elders do not—but they knew of one another.

Uncle Jake taught Harpoon that a weapon naturally cultivates a curiosity in the client. Every buyer has the gun they *want* and the one they can *afford*. This means a customer is always on a journey, moving from purchase to purchase in pursuit of their dream acquisition. Harpoon's job, Uncle Jake said bluntly, is keep them on this path.

The meeting is moving along. One by one, each team member completes her report.

"I only did one cash pickup," Lena announces. "Baby was kicking too much last night, so I couldn't get out there. I'll get it this morning."

"How we doin' on Peoria?" Harpoon asks, referring the team's upcoming trip to rural Illinois to replenish their weapons stock. Every few months, this trip is on the team's calendar, sometimes to purchase weapons, at other times to build relationships with suppliers for future buys.

"I'm trying to get someone who can drive us. I'm still looking," Juni says unenthusiastically. Juni dislikes traveling to rural white communities to purchase weapons. Leaving Chicago makes her feel uncomfortable.

"Damn, girl," Harpoon shakes his head. "Don't worry, ain't nothing gonna happen. Just find me a driver you trust. Why is it so damn hard to find a driver?" Downstate trips put Harpoon on edge. Chicago cops are usually too busy to go after each local gun trader. The one who travels the state, or migrates across state lines, will attract federal law enforcement, who have more time to surveil and capture traffickers. Harpoon likes visiting the rural Illinois farmlands where he was born, but he is well aware that every visit increases the risk of apprehension.

"That old cop, Johnson, is around," Sally says, reporting on the behavior of a police officer in the neighborhood, Jerome Johnson, who has been inquiring about recent gun trades. He's asking around about who's selling and who's buying. That's all I know for sure."

"Watch him," Harpoon says. "Get someone on it." He instructs her to hire a homeless person to snoop around and figure out who Officer Johnson is hitting up for street gossip.

Harpoon then pauses to congratulate everyone on a solid summer. They have sold 80 percent of their stock. No one was arrested. Only one crew member—Sally—faced an attempted robbery, but she managed to run away before the money was stolen. They will each receive a bonus, he announces, with the sum to be announced after all debts are paid off.

Everyone appreciates the news. Gun trading is fraught with danger and no one takes a successful summer for granted. Nobody in the group will get rich from selling weapons—not even Harpoon—but that's not the attraction. While some schemes like bulk drug buys can earn you more cash, nearly everyone who takes a shot does prison time. The group's gun business is more modest and steady. They sell several dozen weapons a month on Chicago's South Side. And gun inquiries mean they are likely to hear of other shit going down. They know who's selling something and who's looking to buy, which lets them charge a fee for putting buyer and seller together.

In a good year, by selling guns and working on side hustles, Harpoon might earn $50,000 while the women can pull in $25,000—all tax free. Year after year the earnings are reliable, the cash in their pocket gives them social status locally, and they don't work for a terrible boss. For women whose only other option is low-wage, menial work, there are few complaints.

Harpoon reminds them to stay focused. "Plain Jane, right? We staying low and out of the way, right?" The women roll their eyes. They know this plain-Jane speech by heart. Keep a low profile. No fancy cars, no fancy clothes, no fancy airs. Harpoon insists that only a plain-Jane attitude will keep them on the streets and out of prison.

Finally, the team talks about upcoming sales—always the final item for discussion. As autumn surges into winter, new inquiries head their way. The post-summer slowdown gives way to a new round of inquiries. Drug sellers battle for teen customers new to drug use. Young gang members prefer to steal cars in the winter— when the sun sets early. Sex workers can offer no consistent reasoning, but winter always means more clients asking for a firearms source. For Harpoon's crew, these rhythms mean new opportunities to sell weapons.

But these new inquiries are not without headaches for the team. The black-market flurry will also lead to a greater presence of local police. The gangs are recruiting new members at school— which means more people they might need to track.

With stomachs filled and menthol cigarettes lit, the team starts to discuss this week's customer inquiries. Missie goes first. Her report immediately catches everyone's attention.

"I got someone who needs three 9 milli's by Friday morning, better if it was tomorrow," she begins. Missie monitors Harpoon's every facial twitch as she continues with her report. "It's complicated. The guy who needs it is running a crew—he's a new boss. I mean, he's really a baby!" Missie laughs in an effort to ease the tension of a request for multiple firearms. She knows what the others are thinking. *Is this legit? Sounds promising, but can this buyer be trusted?*

A three-gun purchase is a rarity and it comes with certain risks. A crafty hustler will often advertise an interest in multiple weapons as bait to attract gun sellers who can then be robbed. For this reason, each crew member observes a soft rule: be circumspect with customers. Deny and deflect the curious at all times. Plain Jane, at all costs.

There are other rules to follow. Everyone must gather intel before announcing a new customer. This means answering at least one basic question: *Is the customer trying to stay safe generally or are they on the run?* Locals tend to fall into one or the other group. Buyers who are caught up in some drama bring extra risks for Harpoon's team and extra information that must be gathered. All of which will help Harpoon to decide: *Do we proceed or walk away?*

Harpoon listens intently to Missie. He motions with his hands to keep going.

"They are selling on the corner, next to the park. The leader is Frankie Paul." Missie reveals everything she knows about Willie's crew. "They are losing business—far as I can tell. He needs it by Friday morning, better if it was tomorrow."

Harpoon can spot Missie's enthusiasm. Her feet tap the ground rapidly. Her mouth draws on her cigarette with small, angled puffs, while she speaks. She wants that commission—likely a few hundred dollars depending on what the customer ends up paying.

Harpoon's job is to be skeptical. "Hold on," he says to her. "Check this new leader—Frankie. He's young, his business ain't so good. He stressed out! Ain't none of us heard about him, right? So what's that all mean?"

"He's probably starting something himself," Juni chimes in.

"Yeah!" Harpoon cries out. "This just don't feel right."

Harpoon runs the calculations in his mind. Three firearms by Friday means a weekend hit is likely in the works. There will be a shooting. Cops will look for the outfit that sold the guns. Harpoon doesn't need the police poking around. He asks Juni to hire homeless men to scour the neighborhood in search of likely undercover cops.

One other detail troubles the team: they've not heard of this conflict before, nor do they know much about Frankie Paul. Harpoon takes pride in knowing the beefs in his neighborhood and the people behind them. On occasion, Harpoon's team may be surprised to find out about a simmering problem, but in a town of familiar faces, they usually can spot the early warning signs of fighting on the horizon. Something doesn't feel right about Frankie and his crew.

As the facts settle, Harpoon believes he has a good idea of what's happening: Frankie is a desperate young man, new to the game, acting on passion, and not very proficient at making money. He wants to make a show of force. Harpoon concludes to himself: *It is not worth taking a risk on such a fool.*

Missie senses her boss's hesitation. "I trust this brother Calvin. He's the one who texted me. He always does right by us," she says excitedly, referring to the prison guard who works with Willie's crew. "We can probably ask $3,000 for three, if they're all clean."

Everyone leans back—a collective expression of *oooh*!

Three thousand dollars is a steep price for handguns. This offer will be hard for them to resist. Whoever pays this sum is also likely to pay this sum again. And again.

Missie does not mention the second inquiry from Antoine. Nor does she reveal that she also learned this morning that Frankie and Antoine are running together with Willie's crew. Disclosing that there are two clandestine requests from the same gang will make Harpoon skittish. Feuds between two warring gangs are difficult enough to navigate. A conflict within a single organization is quite another matter. Harpoon doesn't like to get involved in what he calls "family business"—too many emotions, too much instability. He will immediately decline such opportunities.

Missie has already thought of a work-around for Antoine. She has plenty of guns in her private stash. She will sell Antoine one of her own and assume the risks, even if it means Harpoon will be upset that she sold a weapon to someone behind his back.

"I need to take a walk," Harpoon says. "Most likely we'll let that boy Frankie have one, not three. I never like it when a young buck has no protection. Bad way to start off in this business. But I want to think on it a bit."

Harpoon zips up his leather jacket and starts to walk away. This could be a fifteen-minute walkabout to clear his head or it could be a three-hour amble around Rosewood. Missie and the others check their phones and send word to those waiting. This meeting will be going on longer than usual.

"Heading out west," Harpoon calls back to the team. Harpoon has decided on a longer stroll. He is heading over to Prairie Avenue, a mile away from Holden Park. This is his safe spot. The place he comes when life is too much for him to bear. Today is proving to be one such day.

For Rosewood's gun traders, local conflict is complicated. Any dispute is a potential opportunity, but each must be managed carefully. Greed does not work in one's favor. Sell weapons *everywhere*, and police will notice. Sell *too many at a time*, police will arrest you. *Sell just a few*—like Jonny Isaac and the street hustlers—and you can't earn a living.

Sell somewhere in between and you have a chance to survive.

11

Harpoon makes his way over to Prairie Avenue. On one side of the corner is a gentle line of out-of-business stores. Fraying, decades-old signage announces the remnants of a barbershop, hair salon, grassroots church, dry cleaner, and Laundromat. Along the two-block stretch, each building waits for a new owner who will refurbish and breathe life back into them. Across the street, a gray Cutlass Ciera, black Lincoln Town Car, and rusted-out Ford Fairlane butt up against two majestic but crumbling 1930s brownstones. On the other side, spray paint vernacular turns an alleyway into a makeshift cultural archive: FRED HAMPTON LIVES! COMMUNITY GARDEN #9, CAIN AIN'T ABEL, DISCIPLES BLEED BLUE! And, above, perched atop a thin steel tower, a busted-up Chicago police surveillance camera repurposes itself as a perch for crows and ravens.

At this intersection, everything appears at a standstill. Caretakers and proprietors long ago stopped caring. Surveyors and investors appear infrequently, if at all, and there is no promise of rehabilitation. Even locals no longer cry to be saved. Peering into the future seems pointless.

None of this bothers Harpoon. The past is precisely what he comes here for. This is the corner where his father was shot and killed by a man who suspected that his girlfriend's new baby looked too much like Harpoon's dad and too little like himself. It is the corner where his grandfather preached. It is at this makeshift Rosewood family memorial where his uncle—the one who mentored Harpoon in weapons trading—insisted that Harpoon launch his own trafficking business.

Harpoon began his mentorship not on Chicago's South Side, but several hundred miles away in downstate Illinois. As a young boy in the rural country, Harpoon spent days sitting alongside Uncle T, who was picking up guns that farming families wanted to sell. It was quintessential preindustrial mentorship. A child leaves school at fourteen to observe his uncle manage a small business—a business perfectly set up to pass through generations of family hands.

In the backwoods, Harpoon would sit aboard the family's beat-up brown Ford flatbed truck as Uncle T crisscrossed the region, making his pickups and drop-offs. Rifles, shotguns, pistols, sawed-offs, knives, martial arts gear, and, occasionally, animal traps. Over time, Uncle T turned his sights northward. More and more items ended up on Chicago's South Side. In bungalow, squat, gang clubhouse, saloon, lounge, back porch, and storefront church, Harpoon stayed by his uncle's side. He learned through osmosis the art of managing goods and people in dark, dimly lit, and open spaces.

Uncle T eventually retired and left his Chicago family to settle back down in central Illinois. No sooner had Harpoon reached his seventeenth birthday when Uncle T informed him that he would be expected to take over the business. The vast stretch of farmland is where Harpoon would spend his last few afternoons with Uncle T, just before his murder by an angry customer. A dispute over a five-gun transaction escalated, and the customer decided to use his own weapon against Uncle T, shooting him fatally in the chest. Just like that, Uncle T's careful planning and vigilance, an attitude of caution and resilience he had himself learned from his gun-running father, was voided.

And, just like that, the business was all Harpoon's. No ceremony, no paperwork. The family now looked to Harpoon to provide.

Harpoon immediately recognized that Chicago's South Side was fertile ground. In a few years, he had relocated his business and moved his office to a basement in his cousin's Rosewood bungalow—where there was already a successful drug trafficking operation in place.

Harpoon staked the future of his business in handguns—small pistols and concealed weapons—more so than rifles and semiautomatics. He would discover numerous advantages of the street corner. Adjoining the freeway, the east-west passage made it easy for cars to come and go quickly. The stand-alone, boarded-up brownstones were ideal hideaways—and a temporary shelter—when on the run. The corner bodegas down the block were perfect sites to store his goods and carry out transactions.

Even the down-and-out locals had benefits. Harpoon was most pleased to see older prostitutes working freely on the corner and in the alleyway. Their carefree solicitation of passersby was a sure sign that police accepted the desire of locals to meet basic human needs: shelter, paid comfort, a numbing drink in public space. Harpoon took this as permission to fulfill another basic human right, that of self-defense. In these deserts where men and women fend for themselves, and where the nearest gun store is fifteen miles away, Harpoon would provide them necessary equipment.

In one year, Harpoon became so successful that he moved into his own apartment and began hiring his team. Today, Harpoon stares out at this past with the future squarely on his mind. In six months, he will be a father. He can barely think of anything else.

Harpoon's girlfriend of three years, Cherise, gave him the news over dinner at McDonald's. For no reason, so he thought, she was crying throughout the meal. She kept avoiding Harpoon's questions—*You sure you're okay? Something I did? Anything I can do, baby?*—until he returned to the table with two hot fudge sundaes and a Happy Meal.

"You gonna be a daddy," Cherise cried out.

Harpoon took the comment as more of an existential observation. "Yeah, probably, someday."

"No," Cherise insisted. She set down her spoon and pointed her two fingers at her belly. "I mean you gonna be *this one's* Daddy."

That was that. In a matter of seconds, Harpoon moved from the end of his family's long line of male descendants to a link in the chain.

Waves of anxiety have been enveloping him ever since. He cannot sleep, he has no appetite, and he feels a stranger to his own body. And since that fateful meeting, now a week in passing, he has said barely ten words to Cherise. They've spent most of their time together hugging and crying and eating Big Macs and sundaes in front of the TV.

Every week, Harpoon finds himself passing by this particular street corner. It is the place where he comes for perspective, and for answers to the questions that roll in: *Will I be a good father? Should I keep selling guns or do something different? What do babies eat? Should I marry Cherise?*

And: *Should I tell Missie and the others?* He feels responsible for the livelihood of his team members. They are his family—his only remaining local kin, given that his other relatives are now either dead or have moved elsewhere. Missie and the other women will help him to be a good father. But they also need to earn money. They will worry about their own livelihood when he announces his new status—they will need to know if their business will continue. Managing this reaction and keeping the business running is now on the list of his concerns.

Day to day, Harpoon finds himself distracted. He is having trouble focusing. Decisions are not easy to make. He is aware that gun running does not tolerate those prone to indecisiveness or poor judgment. The market works on performance and displays of resolve. Standing on the corner and staring out at the empty, distressed street, Harpoon has a feeling he is not acting confidently, with a sure hand. Harpoon is right to be concerned. He needs to keep his shit together.

12

An hour after the meeting, Missie finds Harpoon during his walkabout. She knows Harpoon likes to spend time alone, but she is impatient and wants answers.

"So, what we gonna do?" she asks, needing to know whether they will be selling to Frankie Paul. She doesn't hide her feelings. The wind and cold has put her in a bad mood. She needs one of those long bus rides down South. But these days all she can manage is the leisurely cigarette and Diet Coke on her back porch.

Their conversation is halting. Harpoon is bothered. He asks Missie to review the same details over and over. Frustration building in her voice, Missie tries to simplify the decision whether to arm Frankie's crew.

"Willie is in prison. I'm guessing he sent Calvin over to talk to me," Missie begins. "His cousin is Frankie, who never ran nothing on the streets. Now, Frankie in charge. He's scared. I'm guessing someone's coming after their corner. And I'm guessing Willie needs the team to look strong. *So, we gonna give them three or not?*"

Harpoon considers pros and cons of the sale to Frankie. Every gun buyer comes with the possibility of blowback. There's always a chance that the police will come looking for the seller if the gun appears on the streets. The same loop has been playing over in his head. Selling to a teen is much riskier than adults—police and community leaders could come down hard on him if it was his weapon that ended up in a teen gun fight. And walking away from the sale is logical given that Frankie is unstable and likely to attract police attention. But, the money is attractive—and will really come in handy now that Cherise is pregnant.

Risk versus reward. The wrong decision will mean not only the end of a business, but a neatly pressed one-color jumpsuit and a prison cell next to Willie.

For years, Missie has seen Harpoon excel at this calculation. He knows just the right questions to ask—for just the right amount of time—to acquire just the right intel.

But not today. Harpoon is mopey. He can't take his eyes off of his phone. And he keeps complaining. *Damn, it's cold. . . . Why can't you all find me a fucking driver to pick up my shit out of town. . . . I hear we got cops sniffing around again, anyone know why?*

All legitimate concerns and all issues that the team has been discussing for some time, but Harpoon rarely complains.

"Fucking young niggers. I feel for them," Harpoon finally speaks, returning his focus to Frankie. "I want to help this boy. But something don't feel right. You sure you telling me everything?"

Missie answers with a lilt of hesitation. "Well, everything I *know* for sure."

"*Mm-hmm*," Harpoon says. "You say Willie making this request himself?"

"Far as I can tell," Missie responds carefully. She still has not told Harpoon that Frankie's lieutenant, Antoine, also asked her for a gun.

And there's more she's hiding. Like everyone else on the team, Missie takes advantage of her role in the community. People reach out to her for weapons, but they often mention other needs—drugs, sex, an affordable used car, a house cleaner, cheap prescription drugs, a job. She can make hundreds of dollars each month by helping people find what they are looking for.

Or, she can use what she knows to protect herself in the underworld. In the past few years, Missie has been a primary source for a few local cops. She passes on details that could be helpful—like a big drug transaction or an emerging feud between gangs—and in return, the police look the other way when she hustles on the street. This is always a risky venture. Cops can never be trusted fully. And Harpoon could kick her out of the group if he learns of her work with the police. But, as she gets older, she is less comfortable with the risks of the underworld and, if she needs to make a deal with a cop, so be it. With a mother and sister depending on her, Missie knows she must stay out of prison.

As Harpoon considers his options, she wonders whether she should leave or press him to make a decision about the sale to Willie.

Harpoon checks his watch. His girlfriend needs to be at the

doctor in an hour. Her schedule is becoming a convenient reason to make decisions. "*One*," he says to Missie. "Tell this brother we got *one* for him. And you know the drill. If he gets funny on you, just walk away—"

"Right," Missie says, relieved to see Harpoon make a decision. "And if he says cool, we tell him, we *might could* get him the other two? *Maybe?!*"

"Maybe," Harpoon says. "But I'm thinking we don't. We don't know why he needs the other two so quick. What's Willie got planned? Find that out first and then we see if we want to back off or stay in."

Missie doesn't push her luck. She knows Harpoon is right. If Willie is requesting the three firearms, then the ask itself is not unusual. This is routine for an established drug boss. But the urgency is still curious. Neither of them has heard of existing animosities on the street. Until they can answer the question—*Why is Willie in a rush?*—they will agree only to a sale of a single firearm.

Harpoon stares off into the distance. Missie pushes back one more time, but gently. "You sure you okay?" Harpoon does not answer. He has his future on his mind.

13

A mile away, in the western corner of Rosewood, Pastor Jesse sits in his office, a cramped eight-by-ten-foot converted closet in the rear of his church. He gave up his larger and more comfortable space to parishioners needing a practice room for choir. In the middle of a frayed wooden desk, a large black ledger sits open. A soft and worn forest-green bookmark reflects the incoming sunlight. The desk and the ledger are family treasures, handed down from the pastor's father, a spirited, half-blind cotton worker who railroaded up from Mississippi more than a half century ago to start his own preaching.

The sixty-year-old pastor has come to the church every morning since childhood. These days, he arrives promptly at 6:00 a.m. to look over a weekly calendar of church meetings and ceremonies, as well as topics for the weekend sermon.

Pastor Jesse thinks of himself as an "obstructionist" when it comes to young men and women in Rosewood. "I like to *obstruct*. Get in their face. All with love," is the way he explains his technique to the outsiders—social workers, journalists, philanthropists—who come to Rosewood to question him about his approach to combatting youth gun violence.

Most others will see an escalation of conflict as defeat—probably too late to intervene. The pastor looks at it as the fight's opening bell. The pastor will tell anyone who listens that it is never too late. He can stop any person from firing a gun. It's all about getting there in time.

So the pastor tells himself every day.

Today, the pastor's attention is occupied with the left-hand side of his ledger—the page with a wide column and a header that reads "Book of Names." On the page are the names of young men who live in Rosewood. It is the most precious part of the ledger in his view. A young man's name will appear because he is lodged firmly in that *simmering* space. He is embroiled in a conflict that could turn violent and deadly if help does not arrive. This September week finds six names on the page—six young Black men—written in capital letters.

"JAIME been shot at and hiding, BOO-BOO got his 9mm from 49th St. crew, MARLON is looking to buy. . ." Six is not Pastor Jesse's highest caseload, nor the lowest, but it is enough to keep him occupied. At least ten more names will be floating through his head—the result of three weekly sermons, daily prayer groups, after-school street patrols, and evening parishioner meetings. There's always a lot of talk of people ready to settle a score. There are always nominees for the page because there is no shortage of domestic quarrels, bar brawls, and funny looks that reach the pastor because they've taken a turn for the worse. But for any matter to make it into the Book of Names, a gun must be involved and the possibility of gun violence a likely outcome.

After years of listening, the pastor has become a local healer. He can triage the street gossip. He knows where and when, and how, to respond. And precisely what dose of prayer or counsel might keep things calm for a while.

He also knows when a situation doesn't qualify for his book. There are some locals who keep getting drawn to the fire. Like Jonny Isaac, the all-purpose street hustler. Jonny is probably involved in about a half-dozen local incidents at any one time. His name continuously reaches the pastor's ears, but rarely lands on the page. The pastor will eventually run into Jonny, who will accommodate his requests.

The more troubling trend is the young fighter—the teenager or twentysomething man or woman who is unaccustomed to diplomacy. Used to be that the pastor's outreach meant chasing down adults at saloons, workplaces, and gang clubhouses. Now his time is spent rushing off to schools, Boys and Girls Clubs, and parent-teacher meetings. More and more names on the pastor's list are under twenty-five years of age.

Adults can be reasoned with, and diplomacy usually involves separating the parties so that hearts and minds can calm. "Messing with young bucks," as the pastor calls young men and women, is not so straightforward. Two young bucks means two groups of friends, likely two sets of families, and countless others who view themselves as in the know. Conflict brings out lots of voices claiming to be guardians. They all feel an attachment to the youth, and so they want to be heard.

This means nothing is simple. Motivations are not predictable. And negotiating on the streets means being open to unforeseen and unexpected partnerships.

A good example is his work with gun sellers, who are often the first point of contact to stop violence or retaliation. The pastor learned the hard way, a decade ago on one of his early interventions, why this was the first priority. In that initial incident, which now seems from another lifetime, two seasoned gang leaders had placed a $5,000 bet on the outcome of a pickup basketball game. One accused the other of cheating, the favor was returned, and then a fistfight broke out. This caused younger members to shoot at one another from across the court. The pastor took refuge next to a car where he was joined by a janitor — an ex–gang leader — who recognized him from Sunday services. While crouching, the pastor comforted his companion by saying he would seek a gang truce. The janitor laughed and suggested another course of action. "Pastor. No disrespect, but I'm gonna give you some advice so you don't waste your time. There's three people who are selling these gangs all their guns. If you can get them *not* to sell, the truce will happen in about five minutes."

Pastor Jesse felt insulted and responded that he could handle the situation alone. He said gun sales had little to do with gang fighting. The janitor grabbed him by the arm, and they ran across the street together to locate the first gun seller. Over the next four hours, they spoke with all three sellers, obtaining the necessary promises from each to withhold weapon sales to the gangs. The sellers had little choice. The pastor could disrupt their operations with pleas to law enforcement. Normally, the gangs might take revenge on such a person, but clergy are one of several stakeholders in the community—others being block club presidents, elected officials, and former gang members—whom the gangs will not touch.

That evening, leaders of the warring gangs and the ex–gang leader janitor were sitting in the pastor's church, where they agreed to a thirty-day truce. And, no fighting, no retaliation, and no drug sales around the park, so parents could safely bring back their kids.

The next day, Pastor Jesse sought out the janitor to apologize—and ask why the tactic worked so well.

"Explain something to me," Pastor Jesse said. "Why would anyone who possessed a hundred guns worry that they can't get a few more? I mean, why *would* two warring gang leaders, each of whom had plenty of weapons, cooperate so quickly when told their supply lines would be choked off? Don't they have enough weapons already?"

The janitor responded, "Pastor, every man around here is living a 'tomorrow game.' As bad as things are, niggers think it's only gonna get worse. When a man can't call the police, he needs to know he can defend himself. We all got to be able to call someone for help. These gangs depend on those three guys to sell them what they need to defend themselves. If you cut them off from their guns, you're telling them they are good as dead."

No young man or woman wants to be placed at a disadvantage. Not only because they might be hurt. But because they might be ridiculed on their home turf. It was at that moment the pastor understood the motivation of local teens was rooted in a single couplet: fear and shame.

It took over a year—and support from this same janitor—for the pastor to turn this insight into his own brand of street diplomacy. His distinctive approach started to take shape: use every trick to stop the violence, even if it means frightening and shaming the young man or woman into seeking an alternative route.

Now, while others hold public vigils, town hall meetings, and civic protests, Pastor Jesse rushes off to meet with gun suppliers. Others get the public notoriety, the pastor brings peace to the hood.

Today is a good example. As the morning winds down, the pastor heads over to the duck pond in Holden Park. Waiting for him is Officer Jerome Johnson, a local beat cop who was also raised on Chicago's South Side. The two men are coconspirators. At least once a week, they talk about who's messing with whom, and where they need to be to defuse situations. The two have gotten to know each other fairly well. They bicker, forgive, laugh, and get on with their work with ease.

"Before we begin, how come I always go first?!" the pastor cries out as he takes his seat on a bench. Two large oak trees create an intimate overhang. Jerome has brought bread for ducks who happily feed on the crumbs a few yards away at the edge of the marsh.

Jerome calmly accepts the pastor's sentiments. "Okay, fine, I can go first." The officer smiles. "I know we are here to talk about Boozy." They stop to acknowledge the request for help from a young Rosewood gang member. Boozy, who has just reached his limit with street life. He wants out. "I do need your help with him. But I got *someone* else I'm worried about. Another young man. I don't have a lot of info, but I have a bad feeling about the info I got."

"Alright. Wouldn't be the first time you had that feeling." Pastor Jesse nods. He knows Jerome is a slow talker. Details will come, but Jerome likes to take a moment to build a story around the details.

"This girl I work with came to me with something," Jerome starts off. "She received an inquiry for some weapons. She thinks something isn't right. And I agree."

"Retaliation?" the pastor asked.

"No. I don't think so," Jerome says, leaning forward. "Not that I'm aware."

"A crew or just a single person?" A seasoned outreach worker will run down a list, checking off boxes to make sense of the situation.

"A small group," Jerome says, wavering a little. "That's just a guess."

"Okay, a crew. Sort of." The pastor nods. "Has this person ever been in your car before?"

"Nope, nobody on my team knows who he is."

"Is he . . . *right in the head*?" The pastor's final question is often the most helpful. A young man who leaves the hospital or mental ward, or who otherwise has mental health problems, will be more unpredictable and possibly more likely to engage in violence. "Oh, and when is all this going down?"

"Don't know, but I'll find out," Jerome says, pausing as though to remind himself he needs to keep the source of information confidential. "My 'CI.' This person, she thinks it's happening right away—maybe this weekend. *Frankie Paul*. That's the young boy's name. That's about all I got."

The pastor grimaces and considers all he has been told.

"Someone new to the scene. It sounds like the devil got his soul. *Hmm*. Probably could happen any day now."

"Yup, that's what I'm thinking. From what I hear, we got us a boy who is overwhelmed."

The dialogue between Pastor Jesse and Officer Jerome is always a mix of detail and metaphor. After years, what is left unsaid is as consequential as what the two discuss explicitly. Like whether anyone else in Rosewood trusts them to intervene. With years of local outreach under their belt, they have earned their right to butt in when they spot trouble. The two are known figures. There is no more need to defend their presence. Few people ask them to do so.

Jerome has a soft spot for the clergy. Each serves a particular need, depending on their profile. Those like Pastor Jesse, publicly recognized diplomats in the community, become collaborators for the officer in his work to quiet tensions among street entrepreneurs and gang bosses. Others are his CI, who provide intel on what's happening on the streets. These preachers may never sit next to Jerome in a peacemaking effort, but their information will help Jerome gain an advantage.

Jerome takes his turn at spinning the tale. "Here's how I see it. We have a young man, and what is likely a small thorn in his side is causing deep hurt. So, this young man rushes forward when he should stay back. He has no one to help him put the brakes on. He keeps stumbling downhill. Faster and faster. Out of control."

"*Mm-hmm*." The pastor nods, taking in the story he has just heard. *Male, young, reckless, out of control, looking to start some shit*. He is hearing too many of these stories. "Yes, sir, Officer. Sounds to me like we need to spend some time on what *Missie* has brought to you."

"Might be too late, Pastor." Jerome smirks, realizing there is no point hiding the name of his source—*Missie Bateson*, Harpoon's team member. And no point denying that Missie Bateson is now a thread in the story. "Might be too late. I just don't know for sure."

"Okay," Pastor Jesse says, putting on his hat and scarf. "Guess we need ourselves a plan. Maybe we can walk, I'm feeling a little cold sitting here."

Pastor Jesse now has two names. *Missie Bateson*—a source. *Frankie Paul*—a potential shooter. That's plenty to go on. The pastor gently places his hand on Jerome's back. The two men start walking down the path, eventually saying their goodbyes and heading off on their own to uncover more details.

14

Above all else, Officer Jerome Johnson wants to be known as someone who cared. He is sensitive to the struggles for youth in Rosewood. This is his backyard—where he grew up and learned to negotiate the streets. His fellow officers are well aware how familiar he is with the local terrain. *Hey! Look, it's fucking Mayor Johnson!* they will tease him. Jerome takes it as a compliment. Though he isn't so forthcoming, he hopes to run for political office someday. He knows he will have strong backing in Rosewood.

But for now, Jerome is a beat cop. It is a job that fits like a well-worn suit. He takes up any opportunity to practice the traditional art of beat policing—walking the district, pressing flesh, getting to know people. And of course, getting intel on what's likely to be a problem. Officer Jerome does not work with partners. Most refuse. They do not appreciate the fine art of human conversation and, anyway, it is usually too cold to walk around the community. When asked to join him, most of his fellow officers respond, "I don't get paid to have conversations."

Today, Jerome is braving the blustery weather at the southern end of Holden Park. He pulls his car over a half mile from his destination—Samir's bodega at the other end of the park. This lets him take a leisurely walk and clear his head. His shift began at 8:00 a.m. and by 2:00 p.m., he has already calmed a drug addict convulsing outside a liquor store, defused a domestic incident at the homeless shelter, and busted two kids selling pot from their bike near school grounds.

He looks into the distance, toward the other side of the park, a half mile away, where he is headed. There is a large group assembling outside of Samir's. Jerome knows this is the perfect audience to ask some questions about the new kid on the streets—Frankie Paul. He relishes group dynamics. It is a fair exchange—he gets intel, those in the crowd can showboat in front of a cop. If Frankie Paul is planning a shooting, the crowd will likely pass on valuable details. For Jerome, a crowd is an easier forum to navigate—no one will look like a snitch for speaking with him. Jerome's questions let them boast to one another about who *really* knows the community. And, having turned to other sources, like Missie, who have little to offer him at the moment, Jerome knows he needs to be creative in finding out what's happening in the neighborhood. Jerome grabs his coffee, throws out some of his pastry to the ducks idling nearby, and makes his way across the leaf-strewn grounds.

James "Jerome" Johnson grew up in Chicago and attended Northern Illinois College, with letters in football and track and field. He is the son of three generations of police officers. Grandpa was a cop on Chicago's far South Side neighborhoods. Dad worked on a special citywide investigative unit. He never presumed he would be anything else. Graduated with a solid B average, majoring in communications and taking a minor in philosophy, Jerome went straight into the Police Academy.

In college, Jerome was drawn to the existentialists. He still manages a few pages every few weeks. Reading Sartre feels like listening to the blues songs of his grandfather, who migrated to Chicago from Georgia's cotton fields. "Grandpa loved the line 'If it weren't for bad luck, I'd have no luck at all,'" he once told Pastor Jesse, when asked why this kind of philosophy turned him on. "Those French writers always reminded me of that! Something about not holding on to any hope that makes you live life!"

Before heading to the Academy for training, Jerome's uncle— a seasoned cop—told him the key to surviving the force is to be smart and have ideas. Certitude and curiosity. Find a way to mix the two. Otherwise, a cop will get wrapped up in someone else's megalomaniacal vision about how to rule—how to rule the force, how to rule the neighborhood, and how to exert unchecked authority. Throughout college, Jerome worked on developing a theory of his approach to law and order. He wanted to create his own story about crime and criminals.

The opening line of his worldview is a simple one, but it hides a deeper view about street crime. *I succeed as a cop when I can truly accept that making it better often means not letting it get worse.* That's about it as far as highfalutin ideas go.

From this, he has developed a view on street conflict. His first priority when assessing a scene is not to impart further damage on people—don't piss on them and don't shame them. What follows is another simple proposition: Before looking for or suggesting a solution, always make sure the problem does not escalate when you get there. This means accept your losses first. The scene is what it is. You didn't create it so don't feel bad that shit is going down. Cops get in trouble when they arrive and become the judge or the social worker. It's not in the job description to be a therapist or moderator for the disputing parties.

Of course, Jerome knows that preventing the problem outright would probably be best. But all his learning—from books, partners, and elders—tells him to rein in that sentiment.

This same spirit animates Jerome's take on society's rule breakers, whom he calls "our other half." "I do not look at aggression as something to be scared of," he told Pastor Jesse when they first met and began exchanging their views. "I don't care if you're on a farm, in the suburbs, or just around the corner in my neighborhood. You want to feel protected and, as you grow older, you must protect others. Yeah, this gets a bit complicated because you have your worse half and your better half. Devil and angel! Do you understand? Which one gets to do the protecting . . . well that's the rub."

With such talk, his fellow cops have understandably lost patience with him. Some laugh at his meanderings. Others keep their distance. Most tell Jerome they don't know what the hell he's talking about. Those few who are willing to be his partner eventually get frustrated and ask to be replaced.

Drama. That probably should have been Jerome's major in college. He approaches everything like a play unfolding in front of his eyes. For the pettiest display of human suffering to more serious acts of exploitation and violence, Jerome sees actors wearing masks. Get them to change their mask and they just might behave differently. Conflict in Chicago's low-income neighborhoods, Jerome believes, is really not the problem. Thinking in this way is like viewing man as the problem with human nature. It is only a matter of time before two people will see things differently. The promise that things will change is part of every human relationship.

Jerome also does not think guns per se are what's making Chicago so dangerous. Men kill, he will say often, not guns. But "men kill *in story*." Meaning, they come from some circumstance, they obtain a gun, and then they set off to create a new set of circumstances. The officer's job is to discern the first set of circumstances and what they might create *next*. Where did the disagreement start? How long have the people been going at it? What do they say about how it all began? Jerome answers these questions not via formal investigation. In fact, he feels he has failed if a formal inquiry becomes his response to a heated quarrel. No. It is his job to know beforehand what might lurch into an episode of violence, so he can stop it informally or at least redirect the energy.

Jerome's data is gossip and innuendo. His weather report is based on reading the casual, off-the-cuff remarks and speculation that circulate locally. Which is why he walks around. He can take in all the tales of the dark side. And this is why he is at Samir's: to listen to a story about Frankie Paul.

As he approaches the gathering at Samir's, Jerome spots a loud, older man standing in the middle of the crowd. He is shouting and spinning around in a defensive position. He is in an altered state, Jerome concludes. The officer crosses the street and takes a position at the rear of the crowd. He can see people have gathered not to antagonize but to observe. They are voyeurs. The man at the center of their attention is coming down off a high. He has a small busted-up glass bottle that he swings around without much control.

Jerome walks up and stands next to the troubled performer, checks his cell phone, and starts singing an Irish bar song. Everyone's curiosity is piqued. Some chuckle and walk away. They know Jerome's schtick.

The man with the broken bottle looks over at Jerome. He is perturbed: this is *his* corner and Jerome is working *his* crowd. Realizing the momentum is lost, he shouts profanities and walks over to the bodega where he takes a seat on the ground, muttering, "Fuck you, dumbass cop." Samir is in the doorway with his teenage son. He smiles, extends a welcoming hand, and says, "Officer Jerome, please come inside."

Officer Jerome will not be filing a report on this incident, nor will he offer any additional help to the man on the ground. His work is done.

Inside Samir's, patrons line up at the front counter. Cigarette smoke hovers, lime green paint is peeling, the floors are sticky with spilt beer, and the dry heat from the radiator makes everyone sweat. Samir and his two sons sit behind a clear plastic window strengthened by one-eighth-inch wire. Samir has installed several air purifiers in a vain attempt to buffer what lies on the other side.

Customers steadily shout out their liquor selections through several small sound holes. Samir's children stand halfway up the fifteen-foot ladder and pass them down. Apple brandy and Hennessy are today's top requests—neither of which is in stock. Everyone begrudgingly accepts cheap beer and wine spritzers. In the back, frozen pizzas, canned spaghetti, and snacks are selling well. And, in an hour, Miss Mae will pull up and sell homemade meals— chicken, sausage, greens, bread—for ten dollars in the back corner. Samir takes fifty cents per meal. Jerome eats for free.

In the back office, a different marketplace flourishes. An upstairs anteroom is a storage locker for a street gang. They rent the space as a drop-off site for runners who pick up drugs from the southern suburbs. (Samir charges the gang a $200-per-month flat fee). A small, cramped staircase leads downstairs to a concrete room with two mattresses. Lorina and Rhonda, two sex workers, serve their clients here three to four nights per week. Samir takes in 15 percent of the receipts; fees are paid directly to his oldest nephew, who then redistributes shares out on Tuesday mornings.

Jerome has come for another commodity: *information*. He has questions and he expects answers. The deal he offers is uncomplicated and nonnegotiable. As long as he can acquire truthful and timely intel, he does not pry into Samir's extracurricular commerce. This means Samir has to play "eyes and ears," which is easy to do given his centrality as a market maker for all sorts of legal and illicit commodities.

"You track them like I asked?" Jerome asks a local homeless man standing a few feet away. He leans up against a side window, which affords a perfect view of a busy street corner far off at the park's edge. He is too far to make out the faces, but the corner activity is unmistakable: cars drive up and customers extend their hand as the boys on the sidewalk bring small packages of drugs. Jerome is watching Willie's corner.

"I tracked them," says Rodney, the principal contractor that Samir enlists to pass on information to the police. "I tracked 'em, and they don't know it's me. Wasn't followed, didn't talk to any-body." Rodney knows how to talk to a cop. Rodney is the son of a police officer who was shot and killed in the line of duty a decade ago—the loss of his father sent him into a period of deep depression and drug use, from which he has not yet recovered. Homeless, he sleeps in Samir's store at nights to provide inexpensive security.

Jerome laughs. "Always thorough, I'll give you that, Rodney. What did you learn, my friend?"

"I've seen better," Rodney remarks, looking out in the distance toward Frankie's group. "They go for about four to six hours. Then, no one comes around. They always run out of what they selling. Frankie is the one who sits outside or in the car. He don't look too smart, if you ask me."

"Why do you say that?" Jerome asks.

"Well, I mean you got four guys for maybe twenty customers who come around? Why you need that many people? You get too much attention that way. Tells me you don't know what you're doing. And, if it tells *me* that, then it probably tells other people who gonna come after you. He don't seem too intelligent to me."

"Keep going," says Jerome. "I heard he may be in trouble. Is he planning something?"

Rodney points far to the left of where Frankie's group gathers. "You see those cars? Black and the brown one? That's Mo-Mo's group. They been watching Frankie. I think they're trying to figure out when his supply comes and when they got the most cash. I think they gonna hit them soon. Rob 'em for all they got!"

Jerome finds this useful information, and not entirely surprising. For years, Jerome has been observing Mo-Mo, another local drug boss, like Willie, who has built up a successful drug business in Rosewood. At forty years of age, Mo-Mo knows his way around the streets, especially how to get rid of competitors. Frankie is easy prey.

Jerome thanks Rodney and sends him off. He has what he came for—Frankie Paul is in a vulnerable position. Something will be going down soon. Jerome starts making a mental list of the details he will have to send back to Pastor Jesse, who will undoubtedly find all of this useful.

Samir enters the room. He walks up to Jerome with a petite Black woman who has her hat in her hand. "Officer Jerome, this is the other person I told you might be helpful." Samir smiles.

"I was told I'd be paid for anything I got to say," the woman makes clear.

"I don't know nothing about that. Go talk to Samir," says Jerome, who has no interest in discussing terms. "But, since you're here, why don't you unburden yourself and tell me what's on your mind."

"They stocking up. That's mostly what I know. I know a dude who I trust to tell me shit. Those boys gonna get some Glocks. Sometime. Can't say when. And, don't know from who they buying, but I know they probably already got some and they getting more."

"Anything else?" Jerome asks.

"Yeah, they got *beef* with those boys who hang out down the street. Heard it from my niece, Sheila. Yup, they been having *beef* for a long time with those boys that stay over where the homeless people live." The woman walks over to the window and points out at three brownstones across the street—including the one where Marshall and his friends have been spending their evenings of late.

Jerome abruptly ends their conversation before the woman

begins asking him for money. This information is helpful, but it is not specific enough to be trusted completely. And he still needs to know the source that is providing Frankie's outfit weapons.

Officer Jerome uses the information to check another box: he has confirmation that Frankie Paul's group is either planning to defend themselves against an attack or planning one themselves against a local outfit. He is content with the information he has received. The officer turns and walks toward the front door, shaking Samir's hand.

15

Missie leaves Harpoon and makes her way over to the western edge of Rosewood. She has two gun sales to set up—one to Frankie, the other to Antoine.

She stops at a long row of affordable housing that now sits vacant—she lights a cigarette and knocks on the window to alert those inside. The high-pitched screech from the El train on the overhead track assaults her eardrums and forces her to knock loudly. Crouching behind a bush, she removes one of the large wooden boards that cover up the window. She steps gingerly inside over broken glass to see the six squatters who live inside.

The row houses once served as the business center for the South Side Devil Disciples. The SDD leaders had been working out of two neighboring public housing project towers. Needing more room for their operation, the gang leaders made an attractive offer to the row house tenants: each tenant would receive $5,000 for moving their belongings into another apartment nearby. The gang then converted the vacated row house units into their clubhouse and a crack-cocaine processing center. On one end of the block, crack sold twenty-four hours, while the other end hosted nightly dance parties and poker games. The police eventually shut down the mini–redlight district—but local cops admitted benefiting since that small stretch concentrated local black-market activity into a manageable space. Better the devil you know, the cops figured.

The city condemned the twin towers over a decade ago, eventually tearing them down and relocating the families to other Chicago neighborhoods. The gangs left for lack of demand. The row houses were left standing and shuttered. The squatters moved in. Followed by Harpoon's crew.

The row houses are now one of Harpoon's three primary storage spaces for weapons and money—two single mothers nearby rent out their bedrooms to Harpoon for $400 per month to store the team's cache.

Harpoon and Missie saw many advantages to helping the squatters settle into the vacated row houses. Harpoon paid them to fix up the broken windows. They also managed to set up pirated power and cable TV. Once finished, the men became a loyal security force for Harpoon's crew—fifty dollars per month paid on retainer to each squatter, more for special requests.

The squatters created a community garden and beautified the area. This pleased the block club president, who took pity and lobbied the police commander to leave the units as is. Harpoon was also pleased. That little gun and cash storage unit is one of the most secure locations on the South Side. The perfect place to bring customers interested in purchasing weapons.

Since Harpoon didn't need all the vacant apartments for his

team, Missie Bateson took two for her needs. She pays the squatters an extra twenty-five dollars per month to watch over the belongings she keeps there. She stores clothes, family mementos, and her own weapons—two 9mm Glocks, a small Beretta that can be easily concealed, and her favorite, a Smith & Wesson Shield she stole from an abusive ex-boyfriend. In a large box, she stores water and dried goods for a week in case she has to go on the run from the police.

Missie also relocated her side trades to the row houses. The squatters distribute OxyContin that she picks up in rural Illinois—a side hustle she hides from Harpoon, who will view this as bringing on unnecessary risk. The men also manage three beds that can be rented (five dollars per night) by any woman fearing violence from a lover. And in summer, local moms bring over grills and prepare ten-dollar soul food lunches for passersby.

Missie sits in the southernmost squat that Larry the squatter calls home. The group gathers on a bedroom mattress. Breeze through a cracked window sways a dim overhead light. Roaches scatter freely around the floor. But not on the bed as Larry has successfully laid down a long surrounding barrier of rat powder.

Larry brings over a small portable oil lamp and some beers. The glow on the wall reveals a half-finished scene of Ernie Banks and the beloved Chicago Cubs. Larry hopes to finish the painting by next spring.

"I got two customers I'm thinking about," Missie kicks off the meeting. She redirects them to Antoine first. "One is for me, not for Harpoon, got it? Let's do that one first. Young boy, needs something clean. I need it tomorrow morning, maybe the afternoon. And it has to be clean. Better if it was new. What you all thinking?"

Stickie, who cooks meals for the group, reminds everyone that they don't need to travel far to find a weapon. "Each of us is doing work for somebody—painting, fixing shit, putting in a toilet. You know what I mean? All those people probably got a gun under their bed."

"Good thinking, Stickie." Larry applauds. "Someone will sell us something right away." Larry understands the suggestion that Stickie just offered. Each of the squatters works as a handyman for at least a dozen homeowners. All together, the group has a good relationship with at least fifty people with firearms. There is a good chance they will find an available weapon quickly.

Otis and the others toss out names of people who have guns in their homes.

"Old man Joe got a shotgun he keeps under his pillow!"

"Mavis, out on Oakwood, got two sons who keep their pistols in the basement."

"Autry just got home from the army, didn't he? I seen a bunch of pistols in his safe. He was firing out in the park last week. You heard it."

"Miss Morton. She's old. She can't even pull the trigger on the one her son got her! I know she'll give it to us for $500 probably."

Missie reminds them of the necessary specs. "*Clean. Working. Light enough for a young buck.* How do you all know these are clean—or new?"

Larry responds. "These people are mostly older folks, Missie. So, they don't play like you play. Most of them probably bought their gun in the suburbs. Even if they have used ones, they never shot them at nobody."

The group nods. The chances are negligible that these elder Rosewood homeowners and family members have purchased street-grade weapons with questionable backgrounds.

"Tomorrow," Missie says, accepting the logic. "Got to have it by tomorrow. I'll take care of you. But my name stays out of this one, got it?"

Missie checks her phone. Harpoon has been trying to reach her. Something is up. She doesn't have time to talk about the sale to Frankie. She will have to return. "Shit, I got to run," she says. She lights a cigarette and leaves the unfinished pack and forty bucks for the group to cover expenses.

16

Missie walks out of the row houses and is surprised to find Harpoon pulling up in his car.

"We got to go downstate—right away," says Harpoon, taking a seat cross-legged on the hood of a weathered and dented Chevrolet pickup. Harpoon can afford a new vehicle but, in case unfamiliar police pull him over, the aging vehicle helps him keep a low-profile—his plain-Jane approach. "We're running low, need to get more supplies."

Missie does not answer. She is out of breath and once again exasperated. Harpoon is growing more and more unpredictable. *Why is he mentioning a downstate trip again?* she wonders. At their team meeting, Harpoon already mentioned the need to buy more firearms to keep up with local demand.

"You told us this already," she responds

"Shit changed. Gotta act faster," Harpoon said. "I can't really get into it right now." Harpoon does not like talking so obliquely and so brusquely to Missie. He prefers transparency. But he is in a bind and full disclosure could damage his chance to get out.

"What's going on?" Missie says, frustration creeping into her voice. It has been a long day and Missie is tired. "You ain't been yourself, my brother."

Harpoon turns the conversation to the sale of weapons to Willie and Frankie.

"I'm hearing lots of shit about Willie. I hear Frankie got *dust* on him," Harpoon says. Dust. A novice leader, without any street experience. "He ain't been out there. Ain't never pissed off nobody. So why is he out to shoot somebody? Something ain't right."

Didn't they already establish these facts in the last meeting? Missie thinks to herself. She is deflated. She has worked hard on this sale of firearms to Willie's crew. Her plan was to instruct the row house squatters to hand over weapons to Calvin the security guard, who would then turn over the guns to Frankie.

Harpoon keeps talking, "See, here's what I don't get. Why is Willie coming to *us*? I know the brother already got about *forty* guns put away somewhere. Why can't he give one of *them* to Frankie?"

Missie is embarrassed. This is an important—and obvious—point. She should have been aware of Willie's hidden cache.

"Only one reason," Missie says, putting out the cigarette and shaking her head.

"That's right," says Harpoon. "Only one reason."

"Shit," Missie says. "Frankie's *thug-free*! Damn, Willie played that one real nice, didn't he."

"Sure did!" Harpoon laughs, and extends his hand out to Missie. "*Thug-free is right.* Let's think on what we do."

"Thug-free." It's a term of street art among hustlers.

Harpoon believes that Willie knows that his younger cousin, Frankie, has plans to initiate a battle with a rival. Typically, Willie would call off such plans. Any such incident would bring about police patrols, which is bad for business. However, this time, Willie is probably making a different calculation. The incarcerated kingpin may see benefits to Frankie's plans. Willie's bet is that community leaders will be up in arms because local teens are involved in violence. *How could our children be involved in a shooting?!* people will cry. Clergy, parents, outreach workers, and teachers will all put pressure on cops and city leaders to respond. There will be protests in the streets. Church leaders will hold vigils. The local media may even cover the incident.

In practice, this means that Frankie's group will be looked after—*protected*. At least for a few months. All the local thugs who are salivating at the prospect of capturing Willie's territory will need to back off. No gang leader will make a move on Frankie with the cops and the community watching. No smart criminal will risk coming after Frankie if he's *protected*.

Put more simply, a community response will protect Willie's group from a takeover and any immediate harm from neighboring gangs. And such a response, by reducing further violence, means customers will feel safe coming around again.

Frankie will be *thug-free*.

What exactly being thug-free means for Harpoon and Missie is not so clear. They could profit by selling guns to Willie, especially as he expands his business. But doing so may risk community backlash, particularly from outreach workers and diplomats like Pastor Jesse. Alternatively, they could walk away—but lose a valuable client in the process.

"Let's think about it," Harpoon says. "If shit goes down and Frankie fucks up, the cops are coming after us. Man, I really don't need that right now."

"Yeah, but *only* if shit goes down," Missie responds, offering up a counter argument. "If *nothing* happens, then we got ourselves a lot of new business!"

Harpoon knows he should be conservative. Whatever Frankie and Willie are planning for the immediate future, the result will be more cops on the street.

Missie makes a different bet. She asks her boss to consider that nothing bad may happen. In this more favorable scenario, their team could earn three to five thousand dollars, depending on what Willie purchases. That kind of cash is not easy to ignore, especially given Missie's desire to exit and Harpoon's present status as a father-to-be.

Harpoon can sense that Willie is testing him.

"I don't trust that nigger," Harpoon mutters. Harpoon senses that the imprisoned drug boss is gauging his tolerance for risk—specifically, whether Harpoon is brave enough to get involved with Frankie.

"You think he's coming after us?!" Missie asks, not having considered this option.

"That nigger's got a lot of time to think of new shit to do," Harpoon says. "Niggers get ambitious, start dreaming a lot when they locked up."

Harpoon is thinking about his reputation on Rosewood's streets.

Word will travel if he refuses to arm Frankie. People will wonder whether the seasoned gun trader has lost his mettle. Rumors will spread. Harpoon will appear vulnerable, and speculation will follow: *Harpoon has lost his touch. Harpoon is working for the cops. Harpoon is ready to be taken over.*

With fatherhood approaching, now is not the time to jeopardize his reputation and his economic security. Harpoon must earn money for his growing family.

"There's some folks who don't want us getting involved right now," Harpoon tells Missie. His references are unclear.

"Let me guess," says Missie, visibly dejected. "People been calling you. They want to stop Frankie before he shoots up some young boys." Missie's guess is that someone in the community has been meeting with Harpoon. Someone who knows the situation on the streets. Someone wants to preempt conflict by preventing guns from reaching the young boys.

Harpoon chooses not to be forthcoming. Not just yet. Everyone on his team already knows he is not a loner in Rosewood. Cops, clergy, schoolteachers, social workers, all can reach him when necessary. He is a first call when one of these peacemakers needs to keep the guns off the street. Harpoon is a key asset in their efforts to reduce violence. This is a part of his work he discloses to Missie and others discreetly.

Harpoon sighs and raises his arms. He has reached a decision. "Here's what I think. Let's go ahead and get two ready. But we gonna wait for a day—maybe even the weekend just to see if shit cools down. Put the word out that we gonna take care of this group if things start to get bad."

Missie is relieved. At best, she hoped for the sale of a single weapon. Two is a nice surprise. The street will respond favorably when they hear Harpoon is willing to back up Willie and Frankie. Harpoon's rep will be safeguarded for the time being.

"Okay, I'm gonna check on a few things." Missie says, not wanting to upset Harpoon any further. She throws her cigarette on the ground and makes her way back toward the row houses. The weekend is fast approaching. Anything could go down on the weekend.

17

A few hours later, Pastor Jesse walks into Sweetwater, a local bar, taking a seat next to Harpoon. The bartender brings over a glass of milk with ice. Pastor Jesse says a brief prayer and sips from a straw. Harpoon distractedly nurses a club soda.

The bar is nearly empty. The jukebox wails Aretha Franklin's "I Never Loved a Man (the Way I Love You)." Decades of grime on the large front window softens the view of the dilapidated three-story apartment buildings across the street.

The cook peeks out, and Pastor Jesse signals for him to prepare his usual meal—chicken wings, fries, and greens. He turns to Harpoon. "I got thirty minutes. Let's skip the small talk. Tell me what you know about this boy, Frankie Paul."

Pastor Jesse reached out directly to Harpoon immediately after the meeting with Officer Jerome. He knew he had little time to act. Harpoon's teammate, Missie Bateson, broke the news to the officer that Frankie was in the market for a weapon. The pastor now knows that Harpoon is most likely involved with Frankie's gang.

Pastor Jesse will lean on his ten-year relationship with Harpoon, whom the pastor has called upon dozens of times when a local beef starts to heat up. He hopes Harpoon will refuse the request to sell weapons to Frankie, but he knows the best he can hope for is a delay in fulfilling the order.

There is no mystery between the two men. They've worked with each other for years. Harpoon is used to these requests. "Don't know how I can help you on this one, Pastor," Harpoon says. "You know what I know. I never met this boy, Frankie."

Pastor Jesse stares at Harpoon disbelievingly. Very rarely does Harpoon plead ignorance to a matter in the neighborhood that involves a man and a gun. Harpoon is too good at his job to know so little. The pastor tries a different route.

"Well, let's get back to what we *do* know, and see if we can help each other out."

Harpoon orders another club soda. The negotiation with the pastor is easing his tension. It reminds Harpoon of his childhood. As a young teen, Harpoon began traveling with his uncle to business meetings. At that time his uncle ran gambling and sold weapons in Bronzeville, a nearby historic district where Black southerners first came up from the South to escape segregation over a century ago. Harpoon watched as his uncle took control of a conversation, turning the situation to his advantage. The day usually ended with a long walk home in which his uncle gave Harpoon a lesson on doing business in the ghetto. None of it made sense at the time but Harpoon took away some core ideas: Stay close to your customers, particularly if they feel disgruntled or treated unfairly. Always acknowledge their concern. Keep the talk moving and don't commit.

Harpoon was taught to love the process. He particularly enjoyed negotiating with Pastor Jesse. He felt it brought him a little extra favor from the Lord. The softness he felt from the clergyman made it difficult to negotiate, but Harpoon hoped the Lord would reward him for being a reasonable man.

Today's discussion regarding Frankie Paul is an opportunity for Harpoon to flex a little. He knows the pastor cannot let a newly armed young man go on his way without notice or intervention. He predicted that the news of Frankie deciding (with Willie) to arm himself would reach the pastor. He expected the pastor to intervene—which means he would be calling Harpoon for this favor.

"Son, let me tell you what I know," Pastor Jesse says. "I know we got us a boy in some state of confusion. I believe this Frankie is feeling strife inside and is about to do something. I'd like to have the chance to stop a shooting. And, I believe you would too."

"Yes, yes I would," Harpoon says with a laugh. "Bad for business, that's for sure! But, on this one, Pastor, I got to be honest with you. We got ourselves a chance to . . . *facilitate*." Harpoon chooses his words carefully so the pastor understands that he has not yet sold Frankie a weapon. But he needs the pastor to know he is interested.

Pastor Jesse processes the wealth of information Harpoon has conveyed in just a few sentences. He is well aware that Harpoon can call off any deal that is underway. He makes a proposal. "Can I get you to step back for seventy-two hours?" The pastor wants Harpoon to declare a three-day moratorium. No sales to Frankie's crew in that window. This will give the pastor some time to learn more about what's happening with Willie's crew.

"I can do twenty-four," Harpoon responds. Harpoon knows Frankie needs a gun sooner. If he waits three days, he will lose the sale.

"Okay, I'll take it." The pastor expresses a sigh of relief. He has a small window—a day—to stop Frankie from becoming the seventh name in his Book of Names.

Harpoon's cooperation is a good beginning. There are four other pro street dealers in Rosewood who will sell a firearm to Frankie. There are also more hustlers like Jonny Isaac in Rosewood and in the surrounding neighborhoods who are possible sources. There's little chance that Frankie himself will head outside Rosewood to buy weapons. Knowing that a young man will fear moving beyond the local scene to circulate with strangers, the pastor readies himself to speak with the other local gun sellers.

Looking over at Harpoon to say goodbye, the pastor notices that Harpoon is bothered. "You okay, son? Usually you got some fire in your eyes. Ain't seeing that today."

Harpoon wants to tell the pastor about Cherise's pregnancy. He wants advice about being a father. He trusts the pastor. And, with no other adult male in his life, he needs an experienced voice at his side. The pastor would be the perfect person. But that conversation will have to wait another day. Harpoon doesn't want to jeopardize this negotiation by showing vulnerability.

"Maybe we can just talk sometime, Pastor," Harpoon says, staring off into a television set featuring local news at the far corner of the bar.

PART **3**

18

Early Friday morning, Frankie and Antoine wait inside their idling car at the end of a long residential block on the eastern border of Rosewood, about a half mile from the Lake. The morning passes slowly. Their eyes are fixed on a small two-story cottage, the smallest of homes in one of the more upscale corners of Rosewood. Inside the house is Tiny Thomas, their youngest team member. Tiny called Antoine, saying he was too scared to participate in the planned raid. A skittish member is not welcome news this close to a main event. His hesitation could spread to others.

In their practice run, Tiny peed all over himself. He sat shaking in the back seat of Antoine's friend's car with his pants soaked. The fact that he couldn't hold his bladder wasn't really their concern — they could care less if Tiny had soiled his pants. Neither was Antoine concerned about explaining the mess to his friend. What pissed them off was Tiny's big mouth. After this embarrassing incident, Tiny ran home and told his aunt Rose what happened. He also revealed to her the group's plan to go after Marshall. Antoine found this out from another team member.

Antoine and Frankie have questions for Tiny and they need answers. *Did Aunt Rose call the police? Who else did she tell? For that matter, who else did Tiny tell?!*

Chances are pretty good that Tiny also shared the news with his girlfriend, who likely reported out to her friends. So far, Facebook and Twitter are silent. But the two leaders know this won't last for long. Soon, the entire neighborhood will be on notice that Frankie's crew is going after Marshall. Whatever advantage they had from a surprise ambush will be lost.

Antoine is upset at himself. He should have seen this coming. Tiny is fifteen. His mother died of an overdose two years ago and his father has not been seen for over a decade. Tiny has been shuttling around from one relative's home to another. He has no history of violence and he has never been arrested. He wants to be a professional singer and is a regular at neighborhood talent shows. Given that his own mother is unhealthy, Antoine can empathize with Tiny's struggles. In Rosewood, where social services are minimal and the demand is great, Tiny becomes everybody's concern and no one's problem.

Antoine and Frankie run up to the front door as soon as Tiny's aunt pulls away in her car.

"Tiny, we got to speak with you!" Frankie bangs on the door and shouts.

Antoine takes a more uplifting tone. "We ain't mad at you, Tiny, but you can't hide in there forever. We're here to help."

Antoine and Frankie walk around the outside of the house. They spot Tiny in a bedroom, watching a cartoon on the small color TV.

"Tiny, you ain't got to do nothing you don't want to," Antoine waves through the window. "But you got to talk with us. C'mon, Tiny, we ain't leaving."

Frankie pulls out a cigarette and nervously puffs while Antoine delivers encouraging messages to Tiny through the double-paned, dirty window. After a few minutes, Tiny appears in a black, Chicago Bulls warm-up suit. He is morose and silent. His eyes are red and puffy.

"Tiny, who you told about what we doing?" Antoine says softly.

"Auntie Rose," Tiny says.

"Anyone else? Are you *sure* you didn't talk with nobody else?" Antoine asks.

"Lucie," Tiny says, referring to his last girlfriend.

"Anyone else?" Antoine presses gently.

"Lucie told Shanea, who called me. I told her we was going after Marshall 'cause he's a little bitch!"

Frankie throws away his cigarette in frustration. "Tiny, damn, who you *didn't* tell?"

"Tiny, that's okay," Antoine says. "But did you say *when* we doing this?"

"You never told me when."

"You sure, Tiny? You didn't say nothing about this weekend?"

"Is that when we gonna beat them niggers?!" Tiny stands up excitedly. "I'm gonna call Lucie. Man, she was saying I couldn't do it, but I told her I'll *kill* those niggers!"

"No!" Antoine cries out. "Tiny, you ain't gonna say nothing to nobody! And you ain't *killing* nobody. Come with us! You gonna ride with us all day. I don't want to see you text nobody. You ain't on Facebook, right?"

Tiny shakes his head. "No, not no more."

Tiny walks back into the house, grabs his phone, and sprints over to the car, feeling welcomed back by friends he feared he had disappointed.

"We can't trust that stupid nigger," Frankie sighs.

"No," says Antoine, "But he didn't tell nobody when shit's going down. So it's cool."

"So, you think we gotta stay quiet for a while?" Frankie knows well enough to defer to Antoine's judgment. "What do you think we should do?"

Antoine doesn't blink. "We hit them tonight, before anyone else figures this shit out. Got to hit them tonight."

19

Five blocks away, Marshall hears a soft knock on his bedroom door. Lanea, his sister, is waiting for the update Marshall promised to give her.

"So." Lanea shrugs, as Marshall opens the door. "You gonna talk with Dad about what's going on?"

Marshall has no answer. The meeting with his friends has left him without much hope. He wants to slow things down, but his friends want to go after Frankie—armed if necessary.

Marshall knows that his father could be helpful. But how much should he reveal to him? Perhaps he should have mentioned his troubles much earlier. Maybe he should tell his father how excited his friends are to fight Frankie's crew.

"Don't avoid me, Marshall," Lanea insists. "Look." Lanea hands over her phone. It is a text from her friend. They going after him real soon. Maybe this weekend at Boo-Boo's party.

The message is clear to both of them. Marshall's friends will all be at a house party on Saturday evening. And, according to the message, so will Frankie's crew. Word has spread on Facebook that Frankie is aiming to start a fight.

"That don't scare me," Marshall shakes his head. "Like I told you, I'll shoot that boy if he comes after me!"

"Marshall, tell me you ain't gonna do nothing stupid. That's all I'm asking for. I can't let you act the fool. You got a gun, Marshall? Tell me the truth."

Marshall does not respond.

"You got to tell Dad," Lanea instructs him. "He can stop this shit before you get hurt or do something stupid. Marshall, if you don't tell him, I will."

Marshall does not say anything. He grabs his backpack and leaves the house to meet his friends.

———

Georgie and Siron are waiting as Marshall pulls up to the brownstone and lands on the stoop.

Siron doesn't waste time. The group managed to pull together $250 for Jonny from their collective savings. Jonny wants at least another $300, but Siron says his cousin is willing to negotiate. "Jonny says he wants the rest of the money—if we have it."

Georgie corrects Siron. "No. We told your cousin that we ain't got no more cash right now. Ain't nobody working."

Siron shrugs. "I'm just telling you what he told me. He got what we asked for. And he wants to be paid."

"Fuck him," Marshall says. "You can tell him that too." Marshall stares down Siron, who lights a cigarette and walks off.

Time is running out. If what Siron says is correct, there is little time left to turn things around. Now it is up to Georgie and Marshall to honor *their* promise to purchase the weapons from Jonny. Marshall knows this part of the deal cannot be renegotiated. Jonny is a powerful voice locally. If the boys balk, he will spread word that they are *pussies* and too poor to defend themselves. Marshall knows he must go ahead with the buy.

Georgie knows it too.

"I know you ain't feeling what we all feel," Georgie says to Marshall. "But, you know everyone got your back. Isn't that what you wanted? And maybe you should think about watching *our* back. We all with you, and you got to be with us. Know what I'm saying."

Of all the arguments Georgie has made, this is the most convincing. For so many months, Marshall wanted to feel the backing of his friends. Isolation was half his complaint. Georgie was right. He should be grateful that the others would risk their lives for the cause. If he wants everyone to fight for him, he needs to fight with them.

At the least, if they do carry out the confrontation, Frankie and every other bully will know not to mess with Marshall Mariot anymore.

20

Antoine has scheduled the attack for 6:00 or 7:00 p.m., depending on when Marshall and friends will assemble on the stoop. He leaves Tiny with Frankie and heads over to the long stretch of abandoned row houses. Missie texted him to show up there, where he can pick up a 9mm Glock firearm from Larry, one of the row house squatters.

"I ain't gonna say nothing," Antoine mutters as he walks. Purchasing a handgun is another decision he will keep from Uncle Albert. There's a good chance Uncle Albert will force him to quit running with Frankie's crew if he finds out, leaving Antoine few other options to care for his sick mother. But staying quiet and executing an armed raid could land him in prison.

Larry approaches, carrying a large grocery bag and munching on a sandwich. Casually, he places the bag next to a tree and walks over to Antoine.

"I got the cash," Antoine says, about to hand him some rolled-up bills.

Larry shakes his head and laughs. "Now, I heard you were pretty smart! So I'm going to assume you were making a joke. You *were* making a joke. *Right?*"

"Sorry," Antoine corrects himself. He forgot that the pickup and cash drop are in two different places. Antoine must place the payment two blocks away, underneath the large planter on the porch of an abandoned house. This is a rule Missie maintains for all transactions.

"Must be one of those days," Antoine apologizes.

"Well, with what you got, you better get that head of yours on straight." Larry smirks and walks away.

After leaving Larry, Antoine drops off the $500 for the gun. Before going back to Frankie, he has two more stops. First, to a cousin's to pick up bullets and then to Uncle Albert's, whom he promised to visit before the weekend.

When he reaches the church, it takes less than a minute for Uncle Albert to pick up on Antoine's vibe. He knows something is not right.

"Antoine, I'm going to ask you to pray with me. Okay?" Uncle Albert grabs Antoine's cold, clammy hands. Antoine is anxious. Each year, Uncle Albert will hold the hands of dozens of young men who are in this position: filled with internal strife, wishing they could see things straight, hoping for a way out of their mess. Few manage to get out of these situations.

"You remember what I told you last time?" Albert asks. "You're very good at solving problems. And, sometimes, Antoine, when you solve problems, you create bigger ones. I see in you a beautiful young man. A man who wants to do right."

"You gonna make me tell you what's happening, ain't you?" Antoine says softly.

Uncle Albert chooses his words carefully. He recalls his own prayer session, in which he came away feeling that the Lord had given Antoine a test. He does not want to intervene—not just yet. "Antoine, I know what's happening. And I know you want to get yourself out of something. Truthfully, I asked the Lord for guidance. For direction. He told me the best thing I can do is to be with you and pray with you. You understand what I'm saying."

Antoine wipes the tears off his face. "I'm doing all this for Momma," he says.

Uncle Albert holds his hands again. "Antoine, your momma would never ask you to hurt yourself. I'm sorry, but this one has nothing to do with Momma. This one is on *you*. I can help you, but I can't make decisions for you. That's what it means to be a grown man. Pray with me."

The wind howls and rattles the windows of the two-room church. Outside a car alarm wails, only to be drowned out by the sounds of the elevated train overhead.

21

Jay Mariot picks up his daughter after school for a late lunch. For the first time in a long time, the Big Macs lie untouched and grow cold. Lanea and Dad usually will remark at how famished they are and how fast they typically eat. Their meals together are a chance to catch up and spend quality time together, and they always begin by eating the food hurriedly. Fries, burgers, shakes hit stomachs in a rush. No one speaks. Five minutes later, they finally raise their heads in laughter.

Not this time. Marshall is on their mind. They thought of asking him to join, but they need some time alone. Their worst fears have come true. His son, her brother, is now caught up in the streets. Like Mom, who is at home with Grandma praying, they are in shock.

Each feels badly for what has happened. Both wish they had been more forceful.

"I should have said something sooner, Dad," Lanea apologies.

"No, maybe I should've stopped him, like your momma wanted," Jay says. Jay knows that his wife would keep Marshall at home for a few months, but something deep inside tells him Marshall will get through this as a stronger man.

"It was different back then," Jay says, leaning back in the booth and reflecting on growing up on the South Side. "People ran over to help you when you did something stupid. I screwed up, Lanea, but no one would let me *keep screwing up*. Does that make sense?"

"Isn't that what we're doing? For Marshall?" Lanea responds.

"Yeah, I guess so," Jay thinks out loud. "Marshall didn't have no problems, did he, when it was just him and Georgie? You think those *other* boys he hangs with are no good?"

"Georgie's okay, but when they all get together, something happens," Lanea said. "Could be Siron. I think they just want to get back at that boy, Frankie."

"Some things ain't never gonna change," Jay says with a laugh. "Same as when I was growing up. When a bunch of people get together, it always gets bad. That's why your grandma and grandpa always watched when I was hanging out in big groups. Around here, that's how the gangs start."

Lanea listens as Jay combs through his memories and shares stories of cause and effect. She has heard most of these tales before, but it doesn't matter. Dad's voice comforts.

"Marshall ain't gonna just walk away from those boys he hangs with, Dad. You know that, don't you?"

Jay shrugs as if to ask, *Why not?*

"If he does, he's gonna have to fight both of them. Frankie's crew and his own friends."

Jay knows his daughter is correct. There is a risk his son will be shamed—laughed at as a coward among his classmates and friends—if he runs away from this problem.

"You know your momma would never understand that," Jay laughs at Lanea.

"*Mm-hmm*," Lanea agrees.

A plan may not have crystallized for father and daughter, but at least they agree on the challenge facing Marshall. Moving forward means working on Marshall's relationship with Georgie, Siron, and others. But how? Jay and Lanea throw out ideas.

"Maybe I should call those boys' dads," Jay says, but waves away the suggestion. He decides that the other fathers will also believe their sons should take care of their own problems.

"I could go after them on Facebook!" Lanea jokes. Jay laughs, and encourages her not to get involved so publicly.

A half hour later, they walk outside. Jay puts his arm around his daughter, giving her the last few sips of his chocolate shake. They walk back to the car in silence.

22

Frankie and Antoine scan their Facebook and Twitter feeds. The alerts from Facebook and Twitter create a mini-symphony on their phones. They are looking for traces of Tiny's conversation with his friends. If they detect widespread rumors of their raid on Marshall, they may need to rethink their plans for the evening.

The rest of the crew is now in the back of the car. Antoine can see that his teammates' anxieties are rising. None of them trust Frankie enough to have these discussions. On occasion, they have been pulling him aside. *How long do we need to fight them? What if someone takes pictures and posts them on Facebook? You think anybody's gonna get hurt or go to the hospital?*

Antoine is worn out from keeping the team motivated and ready to execute the attack. Through a combination of hand-wringing, promises of payment, and some soft threats ("You don't come, and we'll tell everyone you're a pussy!"), he has convinced everyone to take part in tonight's raid. How everyone will act, he cannot predict.

Antoine tells Frankie he would like one more practice run. He finds a safe, cloistered parking lot behind a local strip mall. He closes his eyes to gather his thoughts and obtain focus.

While the crew busily types away on their phones, Frankie reviews his checklist. Sunglasses. *Check*. Gun. *Check*. Mountain Dew. *Check*. Everything seems in order. For good measure, he places his hand on the revolver lying flat under his seat. He has ignored Antoine's mandate, bringing along a gun that he has had since taking over the group. And Antoine has kept his purchase hidden from Frankie.

Frankie knows only one of two outcomes are likely from the drive-by. If things go well, his incarcerated cousin will be proud of him for *finding an enemy*. Or, Willie will be angry at Frankie's reckless decision to raid an unarmed bunch of local teens, and Frankie will be demoted, physically punished, or both.

It is a risk worth taking. Both outcomes are better than going back to foster care.

At 6:00 p.m., after yet another practice run, Frankie and the crew are finally ready. Better to do so right away to preserve the element of surprise, Antoine decides. He pulls the car out of the parking lot and moves slowly into the oncoming traffic on Stony Island Avenue. He expects Marshall and his friends to already be gathered at the brownstone.

The Friday early evening traffic lumbers along. All around their car is an endless sea of tired faces, leaving work and sitting expressionless at the wheel.

At the stop light, Antoine pulls over into the park and slowly makes his way past the duck pond. He looks over at Frankie and gives him a matter-of-fact fist bump before turning on the stereo and jacking up the volume. Tupac. "All Eyez on Me." Heads nod in unison. Feet stomp and the five men shout out the chorus. The rhythmic jostling inside the car makes for a sharp contrast with the dog walkers and evening strollers who move casually about the park. The music has done its job. Each man is in the zone.

Antoine sticks his hand down the side of his seat and feels the grip of his own 9mm handgun. He has made bigger decisions. No longer will he put his fate in Frankie's hands. *If I got to work the streets, I'm gonna make some real money.* Antoine has come to this realization, and he now accepts the inevitable: He must move Frankie out of the way and lead this group by himself. The first step is to make sure everyone understands that he is in charge. There couldn't be a better time to show his command than tonight.

23

At the brownstone, Marshall and Georgie meet with the team to relay the disappointing news that Lanea refused to lend them money. In reality, Marshall never ended up asking Lanea, since she would likely have told their father about the request. It is easier just to lie to Georgie that she turned him down.

Without a weapon, Georgie asks the rest of the group if they need a new strategy. "What you think we should do?"

Marshall expects disappointment, but instead he finds optimism.

Siron checks his phone and reports that his cousin Jonny is heading over. "Jonny will have an idea. Maybe we can work for him and sell his shit!" Siron says optimistically.

Everyone agrees; they would gladly work for Jonny the hustler, even if the tasks are illegal and dangerous. It is worth the effort to show up next week at Frankie's corner with a visible—*armed*—show of strength.

Sensing the momentum, Georgie says, "We all decided to go

after that nigger," he says. "We ain't gonna stop. Next Tuesday night, we gonna do it. We gonna walk over there, and you all better be prepared for what's coming."

Siron and the others jump up. Fist pumps, handshakes. Even Marshall gets into the act, exchanging jabs with everyone. Once again, the thought of beating Frankie does not seem so crazy after all.

Jonny pulls up in his van a little after 6:00 p.m. Everyone is on their phone, sitting silently on the stoop, texting their friends and posting on social media. Jonny knows it is foolish to walk away from this sale—even if the group lacks the necessary funds. He can sense that this is a gang in formation. He has witnessed this scene play out countless times. Young men, weak by themselves, discover a raw power in the company of others. Jonny makes his living not only finding these groups but taking them to the next stage of their collective life. He can move them from a ragtag outfit into a force on the streets who will sell his illicit goods—guns, fake social security cards and doctor's prescriptions, stolen merchandise—and drum up demand for his ventures. This is the time to be their cheerleader and confidant.

Seeing them sitting in a tight circle, Jonny smiles at the thought this could be his new labor force. A half-dozen hungry young men in his employ means he can finally turn his one-off sales into something more lucrative.

"Okay, Siron told me what's up," Jonny says to the group. "You ain't got no more cash. That's cool. I like what I see. You all are fighters. Am I right? Am I right?!" He raises his voice and puts his hands out.

The boys grow excited. "Yeah, that's right!" They shout and slap his hands. It is clear they need his leadership.

"What you need is someone to help make this happen. And *I'm* gonna do that for you all," Jonny says. He takes out his cigarettes and passes the carton around. "See, like I told you before, I believe in you. Now, who you gonna go after? What's that boy's name? Frankie?"

"Yeah," Siron says. "Frankie and his boys hang out on the other side of the park."

"Good, okay, tell me what you planning and let me see if I can help."

No one knows where to start. The truth is they don't really have a plan. Not a detailed one, anyway. Their strategy begins and ends with "let's head over to Frankie Paul's on Tuesday, with a gun if possible." What would they do next? No one is quite sure.

Jonny looks around at the nervous and uncertain faces. Silence. The situation is worse than he thought. Does he really want to lead these teens—just to obtain some cheap labor? It is a questionable investment. He needs more information. Like, what is the reason for their beef with Frankie Paul's crew? Who among them has any fighting experience?

The stillness of the moment is broken up by the loud rumble of a car heading around the corner. Marshall and the others turn to see a dark sedan come into view under the streetlights. The car is a hundred yards away and lurching forward, stopping, and starting again. The car pops forward and then stops abruptly next to the curb. The driver revs the engine. Then, suddenly, the sedan gathers speed and heads toward them. The alarm on Marshall's wristwatch beeps twice. It is time to come home for dinner.

PART

24

Eight o'clock, an hour or so after the shooting. Harpoon is in his apartment with Cherise, dealing with the consequences. The information comes in hot via text. The first messages arrive from his corner boys—the teenagers Harpoon keeps on payroll to keep him updated on local matters. One reports hearing a single shot. Another hears multiple shots from multiple weapons. A third, known to be cautious, writes ??30, which is their code for "Not sure, still need thirty minutes to keep looking around . . ."

Harpoon's team is expectedly jumpy. For any gun seller, a shooting is the sound of market opportunity—someone will soon need to retaliate while another is under threat. Both will feel motivated to purchase a firearm. The messages from Harpoon's team are unclear—they are unsure whether a weapon they sold is part of the incident, and neither do they identify a chance to make a sale. Harpoon must let the conflict mature a bit.

A few curious messages pop up. Two corner boys have just heard another round of shooting about a mile away. Ain't sure it's the same, one says. Another downplays the connection—old man at the tracks.

Eight thirty, and dozens of text messages later, Harpoon forms a mental picture of what happened. Excited, he texts the rest of his team, asking that they meet in Holden Park in a few hours. His crew is scattered around the South Side, but no one lives more than a few miles away.

Harpoon finishes up his take-out dinner—two Big Macs and two Cokes. Next to him is Cherise, who picks at her food. Her pregnancy has made her continuously uncomfortable—she is nauseous and struggles to find a seated position. Two weeks ago Harpoon reiterated his promise to her. His priorities were to be supportive and attentive. He would not place work above family. He vowed to be a good father. She held him to these refrains by forcing him to spend more nights at home.

Time is running out for Harpoon. He has only a few weeks to prepare for an exit out of the trade. He needs to focus his energies on Cherise and his child. But he knows he must take advantage of every opportunity to earn before exiting the gun trade.

He sends a text instructing Missie to figure out what's happening on the ground. He will meet her at the row houses in an hour.

Harpoon hopes Cherise will fall asleep so he can leave. These days, she is generally impatient. Their baby will be here soon. She wants Harpoon's single-minded focus on her needs. Frustrated, she has been setting more rules—stay home in the evening, let Missie run the business, stop answering the phone during meals. For each rule, Harpoon finds an exemption.

"Let me go out and get you some ice cream," he tells her, finding yet another means of leaving. The rule of staying home allows for

Harpoon to leave when Cherise needs food. She does not resist his offer and Harpoon does not wait for an answer. He grabs his jacket, runs out of the apartment, and slams the front door behind him.

Missie waits for Harpoon at the row houses. Although she lives just a few blocks from Marshall's brownstone, a blaring television drowned out the sounds of the shooting. Like Harpoon, she monitors social media and deciphers messages from her sources. And like her team members, she focuses her attention squarely on risks to the business and opportunities to make a buck.

First up is a risk: Antoine. Earlier that morning, in a rare moment of indiscretion, she mentioned to her sister and mother that Antoine was in trouble. She needed to relieve her guilty feelings. She didn't reveal Antoine's involvement in a planned assault, only that Antoine was running with a gang. She needed to speak with someone. Her mom understood and called Uncle Albert, whose church she visits, to pressure him to pull Antoine out of the gang.

Missie knows the situation will soon be getting worse for Antoine. Her hope was that the gun she gave him would help him to avoid any trouble. From the look of the texts hitting her phone, her approach failed. Frankie's competitors are busy contacting her. Bloodthirsty to take over Frankie's spot, they want to purchase firearms from Missie. They tell Missie they will buy whatever she has in stock, at a premium price. Frankie occupies a valuable spot of land. This means any smart gang leader must arm the group not only to successfully push Frankie's crew off the corner, but to then fight off the other competitors making their own effort to claim the spot.

Harpoon pulls up to Missie. "What you hearing?" he asks.

"Nothing," Missie says. "At least nothing for sure." She and Harpoon know that in the aftermath of a shooting, the news that circulates locally will be conflicting. People will share stories about what happened, but not every report will be reliable. The need to pretend one has privileged intel makes people willing to exaggerate—or lie—to elevate their status.

"Look," Missie says, "Shit is blowing up on this one." She shows him the messages of one Facebook group. The gossip appears far-fetched, but the commentary points toward Frankie's leadership.

> You hear that Frankie shitted on himself and couldn't even be in the car with them niggers?! Heard that pussy had to get out of the car and run into the park!

> Man, I heard those boys stripped Frankie naked and beat him good!

Missie and Harpoon follow the exchanges on Facebook and Twitter. In addition to picking up information on the shooting, they are gauging the community's response. They watch for signs indicating that community leaders will be walking through the neighborhood reaching out to youth to understand who was involved and where the weapons came from.

Nothing yet.

Missie still hasn't had a chance to ask Antoine if he was one of the shooters.

If Antoine used the gun during the evening incident, Missie will need to be prepared in case the police track the weapon to her. She knows this is one of those occasions in which being an informant for Jerome could be helpful.

She shows Harpoon the texts she is receiving from the other gangs in the neighborhood. What you keeping? What can I get now? One local gang leader is desperate to know how many weapons Missie can sell.

3-24. A local leader of a drug crew wants three weapons in the next twenty-four hours.

Missie will be busy staying in touch with Frankie's competitors throughout the night. One thing appears clear: Frankie is ready to be plucked.

25

Four white and blue Chicago Police Department vehicles sit observantly at the northern entrance of Holden Park. The cars draw the occasional glance of the ballers on the court and the women tending the community garden. A few yards away, people slowly walk by the old brownstone to see if they can catch a glimpse of evidence. A day has now passed since the drive-by attack on Marshall and his friends. People are on edge.

All around, there is talk of last night's violence, as well as speculations of what lies ahead. Officer Jerome and Pastor Jesse make their way through the park in an effort to listen and record the community's sentiment. Eyewitness reports agree on some of the details of Friday evening—a car drove by, men inside shot at the group sitting on the brownstone stoop, there were more shots, and then the car drove off. But that's where the consensus ends.

And the mythmaking starts.

Consider these four conflicting recollections, collected by Officer Jerome and Pastor Jesse:

1. "Frankie and them niggers got out of the car and started their beatdown! We was across the street and I saw a whole bunch of folks just come out with bats and shit, it was nasty." —*Willa, a friend of Marshall and his sister Lanea*
2. "It was over in about five seconds. They shot and drove away. No one was fighting." —*A squatter*
3. "I saw one of them young boys fire back and hit the car. That's why the car was making all them funny sounds when it drove off." —*Block club president, who was outside walking her dog*
4. "Jonny took that gun out of his pocket. Oooh! You should've seen that nigger run down the street trying to pick off someone in that car! Ain't seen him move so fast since they chased him for shoplifting about a year ago!" —*A local resident*

Jerome himself gathered about two dozen of these accounts, many of which diverged from one another. Good police training tells him to expect discrepancies. And to pick them apart. He starts by looking at the environment. Temperatures on Friday were seasonable, with no visual obstacles like rain or snow. It was the start of the weekend, so plenty of eyewitnesses out and about. The incident took place near benches where people frequently gather and joggers pass. Everyone in the vicinity would have benefited from fairly good street lighting.

Next up is pure self-interest. Jerome expects a mismatch between what a person sees and what they *want* to see. Bystanders love to play the part of color analyst. Most often, people disagree on the likelihood of retaliation and the form it will take. But Jerome finds scattershot remembrances of nearly every aspect of Friday night's event. People do not report the same number of people involved nor how many shots were fired—even basic details like the number of cars participating in the shooting varies among eyewitnesses.

None of this really bothers Jerome. It is worth pointing out why.

There are two types of police officers that will respond to shootings in Chicago's poor neighborhoods. Investigative officers will focus on just the events for a limited period of time—just enough to find a perpetrator, make an arrest if necessary, and move on. Since no one was killed, there is not a high level of urgency. They'll be out of the area in a few days.

Jerome is not one of these cops. He is not here to solve the crime. He is a beat cop who will be hanging around long after the shooting is resolved. He will be concerned with retaliation and the way the shooting might attract other gangs looking to takeover Frankie's outfit. For this reason Jerome keeps searching for the story the young men are weaving about the evening. For it is the story they tell themselves that will shape their decision to keep on fighting—sometimes long after an initial incident.

In practice, on the streets, one hand washes the other and the two cops work together. Investigating officers rely on Jerome and other beat cops to solve problems off-the-books. All agree nothing good happens when teens enter the justice system. Jerome uses this discretion wisely. He will help Marshall, Frankie, and their friends, but he must take care not to put them—or the public—at risk by doing so.

Both Jerome and Pastor Jesse are similar in this regard. Both must move beyond the facts of the particular event to find the myth that motivates people to get back on the street and fight. Both know that the story—the myth the youth use to make sense of things—is his best chance to move them away from the path of retaliation. If the two can change the script in a young man's head—say, from *I have to retaliate to prove I'm a man!* to something like *This is my chance to get out!*—he and the pastor have a shot at making things better.

Jerome and the pastor pause their walk to debrief and discuss what they've heard so far. They take a seat at their favorite bench, a few steps from the duck pond where they will usually find one another. Jerome is in plain clothes—jeans and a button-down gingham blue shirt, with no badge or gun visible. The pastor sports a brown suede trench with a feathered felt hat that puts him squarely in the mid-1970s. This is their preferred uniform for mingling with the crowd.

"All set for the *bubble*?" Pastor Jesse says. "Let's pray the *bubble* holds." The bubble is their way of signaling that their first priority is to shield young ones from further shooting.

"Something concerning you about the plan?" Jerome asks.

"Something always concerns me about the plan when it comes to these boys," the pastor mutters.

It isn't easy to create a bubble that protects young ones from the dangers of the street. The success rate is low. A young person does not sit at home while caring adults engage in street politesse. Teens and young adults struggle with waves of anger, frustration, and shame, all of which fuel the fire to go out and seek honor and revenge.

"Fair enough," says Jerome. "You start with Marshall, and I'll see what I can learn about Frankie and Antoine." Officer Jerome gets up, places the weekend *Sun-Times* newspaper next to the pastor, and walks over to Samir's to start asking questions. The pastor throws the rest of his bread crumbs forlornly on an empty patch of dirt at the edge of a small pond.

26

"Willie's pissed off," Calvin begins, walking up to Frankie at the lakefront. Calvin situates his large frame on the rotted wooden picnic bench. His voice is soft, and Frankie strains to hear his words amid the waves crashing into the rocks. Calvin can tell Frankie is lost. "*Protected*. You're probably protected. Do you understand what *protected* means? Anyone explain this to you?"

Frankie shrugs.

"Around here, Frankie, when shorties like you do stupid shit — like what you did, all sorts of people get involved. See, they want to stop more stupid shit, more kids from getting hurt. Understand?"

Frankie shrugs again and shakes his head.

"Man, I ain't got time to explain everything to you. Listen, you getting double the product this week. And next. You got to step it up. Get everyone out in front of the house. Full time. Push the weed and the coke. Make deals, give it away for free. Willie don't care. He wants to see customers coming back right away."

"Thought I was in trouble," Frankie asks meekly. He is confused. If Willie is upset about the attack, why is he handing over more responsibility to Frankie by expecting him to sell a greater amount of drugs?

"He *is* pissed," Calvin corrects him. "You need to do right. This is your chance to show Willie you made a mistake, but you ain't no fool."

Frankie wonders what he did wrong. Sure, the attack wasn't the smoothest operation, but none of his men were arrested. They beat the other boys up pretty badly. And they all seemed fairly excited afterward. Even Tiny, the one who peed on himself, seemed more confident than usual. So, what was his *mistake*?

Calvin delivers another surprise. "Antoine's gonna be in charge. You gonna need to listen to him, And don't call Willie or go and see him. He'll beat your ass if you do. Or I will. You got that?"

"Why Antoine?!" Frankie asks incredulously.

Calvin shakes his head. "Frankie, no more surprises, okay? Just keep things moving until Antoine takes over."

Calvin decides to leave a few details out in his report to Frankie—perhaps most important that Antoine will take his place in the next twenty-four hours. Frankie has heard enough bad news and Calvin needs to first meet with Antoine privately. He will call Frankie afterward.

As Calvin walks away, Frankie can't help but think about his future. One troubling thought comes back: *Maybe I'll have to go back to foster care and live with another family?* His current situation— shacking up in a house with Willie's extended family—is all based on Willie's kindness. He can accept being dethroned. He never wanted to run a gang or manage a drug business. He considers his options—returning to foster care and cycling between distant relatives, increasing drug sales to make Willie happy, visiting Willie in prison once again to plead for help. Nothing feels right. He gets the feeling that Willie, having saved him once, will not do so again.

He needs someone to counsel him. Unfortunately, the one person who will give him sound advice—Antoine—is the one person he can no longer ask. His best friend has become his rival. And likely his new boss.

27

Later that day, Calvin talks with Antoine outside the house that the crew uses for their drug sales. He needs Antoine to understand the responsibilities of being a crew chief. To this point, Antoine has been insulated from Willie. No longer. He will be receiving direct orders from the incarcerated boss.

Matter-of-factly, Calvin reads out the same rules to Antoine that he recited to Frankie months ago.

"A few things you need to know, Antoine. Never go and see Willie, dig? You call me, okay? I'm gonna give you a code for the phone. Use it when you're in trouble. There's another code for when it ain't no big deal and you just need to talk. In a few days, I'll tell you how to deal with other shit. For now, just do what Frankie says. But then it is all you. Any questions?"

Fuck yeah! I got questions! Antoine wants to shout. Instead, he just nods in silence. None of this is what he expected. He was hoping to meet Willie and get answers to the questions that have been running through his head since he joined the group: *Who are their competitors? What does Willie expect of Antoine? When is Willie supposed to return?*

Antoine feels defeated. He failed to anticipate this outcome. He had imagined being the leader, but on his own terms and at his own pace. He had envisioned a meeting where he would present Willie his vision: *I'll do this for one year, and then I'm out!* Willie would then show his gratitude for Antoine's steady hand. Instead, Antoine finds himself staring at an oversize twentysomething go-between, who is chain-smoking and coughing and delivering Willie's instructions. None of this was in the plans he had drawn up in his head.

"You doing alright? You got questions?" Calvin asks.

"They gonna come after us. What's Willie gonna do about that?"

Calvin can tell he's no longer dealing with an inexperienced teen like Frankie.

"I don't know what you were thinking," Calvin shakes his head. "You brought on a lot of heat by rolling up on those boys. Wasn't any need to start shooting, either. That's where you fucked up. Should've just had a beatdown. But you started shooting. Man, that was a wrong move."

"Wasn't me who started shooting. It was Frankie," Antoine responds quickly. But even he knows that this is an inadequate answer. It was his job to prevent *any* shooting from happening. He should have checked Frankie for weapons before the raid. He should have made sure that there were no guns in the car. He knows it is his fault for ignoring these details.

And Calvin reminds him of it. "Willie knows you put this whole thing together. You fucked up, Antoine."

"Who's coming after us first?" Antoine asks.

"Don't know. Probably Mo-Mo or Vice Lords," Calvin says. "Not to worry. You gonna be ready. Willie is putting the word out today. We gonna find you what you need."

Antoine doesn't want more guns. He had hoped the attack would convey the opposite message to competitors: *Leave us alone!* Instead, it appears to have attracted rivals. But this reaction is not a total surprise. Even he can understand that people view the attack not as a signal of the group's capacity for self-defense but rather their complete incompetence.

Antoine starts to accept that he will soon have more responsibility. And he is now being charged with preparing his crew for what is likely to be an armed engagement with dangerous gang rivals.

"You doing alright?" Calvin asks, seeing that Antoine is deep in thought.

"Yeah," Antoine responds. "Just wasn't supposed to play out like this."

"Never does," Calvin laughs. "That's why you got to look out for yourself. That's what I learned. Take care of your own shit, don't worry about nothing else. You seem smart enough to understand that, my brother. And Willie is giving you a second chance. Don't fuck this one up. You'll be sorry you did."

Calvin walks away. Antoine looks at the texts on his phone. Uncle Albert has been messaging him repeatedly. They were supposed to meet an hour ago. Antoine takes a deep breath and starts walking over to the church.

SUDHIR VENKATESH

On his walk, last night plays back in Antoine's head in sharp images. It started off as planned. Antoine drives the car down the street and stops in front of the brownstone. Frankie and the others in the back seat dive out of the car and rush the stoop. The beatdown seems to be taking off smoothly. They overpower Marshall and his friends, most of whom seem unable to fight back. Then, unexpected events. A team member, Booty, has a large rod—like a sawed-off baseball bat—and starts to beat Marshall's friend.

How the fuck did he get it in the car without me seeing? Antoine wonders.

Marshall and his friends are stunned and half-paralyzed. They react weakly and fall to the ground, where they start receiving kicks to the head and body by Frankie's crew.

By this point, Antoine is looking over his back as he drives down the street to make a U-turn in front of Samir's.

That's when someone starts shooting. As he completes his turn, Antoine can see his crew sprinting back to him. They look scared. Tiny is waving at Antoine to drive back quickly. Someone else is shouting out, "Nigger got a gun! Nigger got a gun!"

Antoine pulls the car over so everyone can jump in. Then, to his surprise, he sees Frankie stop, turn around, and pull out a small handgun. Frankie starts to return fire. *Why?* Antoine wonders. Why did Frankie shoot when his crew was practically back at the car and ready to take off? What made him do that?

There are sounds of broken glass from bullets penetrating a window of the house a few yards away. Antoine crouches down and starts yelling at everyone, "Get in! Just get in!"

Then more shots from another gun, Antoine concludes. Bullets

182

fly everywhere and pierce through another window, shattering glass. No one is hit by the gunfire, but Antoine knows the shouting and the broken glass will bring out the locals. Finally, Frankie pulls open the passenger door. He is breathing heavily, and his hands are shaking.

The Friday incident ends as Antoine speeds away on a side street. As he reaches a safe distance, waves of anger swell up inside him. He can tell the others on the crew feel the raid was a success. They begin their celebration, but Antoine is lost in his thoughts. The sounds of the shooting reverberate through his head. The police will be looking for them. He feels disgusted. He had so wanted to avoid leaving evidence or escalating the incident beyond a straightforward physical assault.

Antoine prays that no one on Marshall's crew has been hurt by the gunfire. He drives the car over to the lakefront and jumps out to grab some fresh air. The others are outside looking through a stolen wallet, laughing and exchanging high fives.

Antoine feels his breath quicken. *No robbery.* That was the deal. He is too upset to shout at his team. Frankie walks off to the shoreline and hurls his weapon into the crashing waves of Lake Michigan.

Frankie then goes back into the car and pulls out some Hennessy from his pack and passes it around. Jubilation, fist pumps, and shouting follow.

For everyone but Antoine. He leaves them to return the car to his friend. All he can think about are the consequences. The police will soon discover the evidence—like the rod used in the beating. Willie will be sure to punish them for bringing out the cops. Then, there is Uncle Albert, who could pull Antoine out of the gang. And what about his own mother—what will she do upon learning what happened?

These are the questions haunting Antoine in the aftermath of the incident. The raid feels like a sore itch. Antoine knows he should move on—what's done is done—but he can't stop thinking about what went wrong and what he could have done better.

28

For Marshall, the days after the Friday incident pass slowly. The images of that evening are fresh in his mind. The tires screeching, Frankie's crew flying out of the doors. The cackles and shouts of the teens as they rush the stoop. Marshall and his friends are slow to respond. They try their best to run down onto the grass and away from the stoop, but they are met with punches and kicks from all sides. What looks like a sawed-off baseball bat swinging widely lands squarely on the back of Marshall's legs—he protects his head by curling up in a ball. His friends are either swinging furiously or on the ground kicking into the air. One of them will have a wallet full of cash stolen out of a back pocket.

Jonny Isaac—the only adult among them—comes to their aid, running over to his van and returning with a pistol that he shoots into the air. "Get the fuck out of here!" Marshall hears Jonny yell. The shots startle Frankie's group, who take their final swipes and kicks turning toward their car.

Then, suddenly, another round of shots from Frankie's crew flies above their heads. Marshall hears broken glass from a neighbor's house and flattens his body on the ground. He feels blood dripping from the side of his cheek where a punch landed. From the ground, he watches the invaders pile into their car and drive off on a side street.

Marshall returns home from the shooting, and Jay and Joycie rush him to the local hospital. An ER doctor, accustomed to seeing local youth in such condition, tells the family that Marshall's pride will be hurt longer than his physical wounds. He is patched up and sent home.

On the car ride home, Jay is beaming. He congratulates Marshall. "You're a fighter, son. Don't forget that." A wave of relief overtakes him. For a few days, his son will feel the bruises. But, after that, he can hold his head up high. If, as Lanea told him, Marshall is being ridiculed online at school for being a coward, this incident should be his antidote. Other youth won't talk shit about Marshall being a pussy anymore.

Jay's posture startles Joycie, who reacts by telling Marshall he will return home to an indefinite curfew. "You gonna sit in that room of yours so you can think about how stupid all this is, and how lucky you are to be alive."

Arriving at home, Marshall is flush with emotions. His face and legs hurt, but he feels rushes of adrenaline. His travel is now restricted to school, church, and home. This leaves him with plenty of time to think. And text. At all hours, he observes the rush of the chatter on social media. People are surprised that Marshall's friends fought with their tougher rival. No consensus on Marshall's personal bravery, but at least he isn't seeing insults.

The following day, Jay takes Marshall to McDonald's, their place to huddle.

"How you feeling about what happened?" Jay says, after a few minutes of silence interspersed with sounds of chewing. Neither knew precisely how to open up this father-son check-in. But Jay is eager to affirm his son's bravery.

"*Hmmm.* Okay, I guess," Marshall says, head down and stuffing fries in his mouth.

"You worried?" Jay asks.

"No, not really," Marshall mutters.

"You planning something?" Jay asks.

"Probably. You think I shouldn't?" Marshall asks.

"I was young, like you. I know what you feel. I probably would beat the shit out of that boy," Jay says.

"Yeah," Marshall nods. "That's probably what I should do."

"You stood up for yourself," Jay says. "You should be proud."

"My friends are even more pissed than me," Marshall says.

"Just remember one thing," Jay says, before clearing the table and rising. "Sometimes, it's just a good thing you did something. Don't matter what you did. You understand?"

Marshall is silent.

Jay is having trouble being direct. Marshall put up a good fight, but Jay knows his son feels the need to defend himself after the incident. He wants to give Marshall one piece of advice: *Keep it a fistfight. Don't get a gun.* But Dad worries these words will be just the reason Marshall decides to be armed for the retaliation. So, no more words are spoken.

Jay puts his arm around Marshall and says they should probably pick up some sundaes for Mom and Lanea before heading home.

The visit to McDonald's with Dad was a high point for Marshall, but since then, Marshall feels the pressure of doing something about Frankie. Despite the fact that he stood up for himself, the talk in the neighborhood is that his friends have yet to respond. His confidence is undermined by the posts Lanea shows him from a secret Facebook group.

> Those niggers ain't gonna do shit to Frankie.
> Bitch-niggers.
> Frankie coming back for Round 2!

Marshall feels the need to resolve things once and for all with Frankie. But what exactly the resolution might be is still not so clear. Dad has been comforting, which Marshall likes, but he hasn't helped him think about how to get Frankie out of his life. By contrast, friends of the family breezily offer up opinions and advice. People continuously visit the house unannounced and declare their intention to be helpful. As the news spreads across the neighborhood, uncles, aunts, and cousins tell Marshall how he should act. But no one listens to what *he* wants. They just order him around. There are too many voices in his head to think straight. As more people come to the house, Marshall hides away in his bedroom.

Marshall is committed to making a response. And so are his friends who were beaten up by Frankie's crew. Via text, they have been rallying one another from their respective homes—like Marshall, the others are under curfew. Each of them vows to return the favor to Frankie Paul. Frankie has underestimated their resolve, they cry. They need to squelch the rumor traveling through social media and school hallways that they are *pussies* who will not retaliate. They cry out for revenge. But what exactly they should do, no one knows.

29

It didn't take long for Jonny Isaac to regret some of his decisions. As soon as the car holding Frankie's crew drove away from the stoop, he began kicking himself for getting involved with Marshall and his friends. He wished he had never tried to sell them a weapon. The group was not ready to be armed. And they were not ready to become the young workers he needed to jump-start his business. He was blinded by his ambition.

He does give himself credit for quick thinking on the night of the shooting. His reaction averted further damage. But it also put him at risk. To a bystander—and more importantly, to a cop— Jonny looks like he is the new leader of Marshall's set.

Just like that, the identity he has worked so hard to create in the community, that of an independent street hustler making a living, shifts to Rosewood gang leader. Any old fool could tell you the folly of Jonny's actions—with the warning shots he fired into the air to scare Frankie's crew Jonny likely permanently jeopardized his ability to make a few bucks on Rosewood's streets. The investigative officer could now take "Jonny the Gangbanger" off the streets and parade him around as a sign of good police work.

And sure enough, the day after the shooting, Pastor Jesse met Jonny in the park and escorted him to the police station. Voluntarily speaking to police would help make the case that Jonny should be given a lenient penalty. In the end, it helped the pastor negotiate favorable terms. Jonny must turn in *all* his weapons to the police, foreswear firearms sales forever, and leave Rosewood for a year. In return, the police will go easy on the hustler and not press charges. The investigating officer will portray Jonny as an innocent bystander who shot into the air to break up the melee and scare off local kids.

Smart enough to spot a favorable deal, the following day, Jonny dutifully packed up his van and drove south to Gary, Indiana, to shack up with a cousin. On his way, he met with Pastor Jesse's social worker, who took all of Jonny's weapons and turned them in to the police. Neither Jonny, the pastor, nor the police made much out of the time period of his sentence. Even if he stayed away for five years, local cops could disrupt his operation for no reason.

Jonny knew that his time in Rosewood had come to an end.

30

In the four days since the Friday night attack, Pastor Jesse's phone has been buzzing with texts, calls, and voicemails from his team and sources in the field. His work began several hours after the incident, with an in-person meeting of his outreach workers. He instructed two of them to gather more information so they could anticipate a retaliation. He sent one to speak with local prostitutes and he dispatched the other to the hospital. Sex workers and emergency room personnel are logical people to visit to learn the basics, including who is injured and who is on the run. The pastor also has his own private list of locals he will call—homeless men, squatters, Samir the bodega owner—to reconstruct the incident. On it goes until his team can gain the trust of local gang leaders who are most guarded with their information.

The pastor then moves about Rosewood to identify and shut off several supply lines for guns and ammo. This best chance of defusing tensions begins by not letting Frankie's or Marshall's team purchase more weapons. Of the professional traders who are candidates for gun sales to Frankie and Marshall, Pastor Jesse quickly obtains agreements from two. They promise to forgo sales for forty-eight hours. This leaves Harpoon, whom he will speak with next.

He also cannot ignore Rosewood's amateur hustlers—like Jonny Isaac—who could make a one-off firearm sale to the teens. Finding each of them is a maddening task, for they live out of their cars, in homeless shelters, and at friends' homes. Better to stick with the pro dealers and use the amateurs sparingly for intel.

Next up are the meetings with parents whose children were involved in the shooting. His first stop is to see Jay and Joycie Mariot. The pastor stops by the Mariot household on Monday, when Marshall is at school.

"I heard your son and his friends are looking for a 9mm." Pastor Jesse greets Marshall's parents at the front door of their home. His outreach workers know that Georgie has been putting out a call in the neighborhood for firearms.

"How the hell can we stop him?" Joycie says, startled at the news.

"You can start by inviting me in," Pastor Jesse smiles, as he puts his face up to the screen door. Jay laughs, opening the door and shaking the pastor's hand.

When they reach the living room, the pastor keeps talking— borrowing a line from his friend Officer Jerome. "We need to talk to your son. See, young people like to tell stories to themselves. It's how they make sense of the world. If we don't know his story, we won't know how to get him to tell a different one. But, first, let's get to know *your* story. Tell me something I don't know about your family. About Marshall."

Jay and Joycie look at one another. Neither knows precisely where to begin.

"We've never really thought about Marshall's *story*." Jay sighs. "He's an ordinary kid."

There is that word again. *Ordinary*. Jay says it proudly. The pastor knows exactly what he means. Far be it from him to laugh off the achievement of raising an *ordinary* kid in these neighborhoods.

Neither Jay nor Joycie understand completely what the pastor means by discovering Marshall's "story." But they are open to any effort to help their teenage son—who is usually in a semimute state, hidden away in his bedroom, when at home. Their own conversations with Marshall have been curt and mostly monologues. Most of their exchanges go like this:

"Marshall, what did you say to that boy to make him come after you? Why is Frankie so upset at you?"
"Don't know."

"Did you steal something from him?"
"No."

"So, why would he come after you?"
"Don't know."

"Is there something you aren't telling me?"
"No."

It takes only a few minutes for the pastor to give Jay and Joycie his diagnosis. "I have no doubt that Marshall will soon purchase a gun. If I were him, I would too. He's tired. He just wants to end his misery. That usually is what drives these young men to shoot back. That, and friends who feel the same way."

"We have to stop him from buying a weapon!" Joycie cries in disbelief. She is visibly embarrassed that the situation has reached this point, and anxious that it could get worse. "I'll make sure he doesn't have any cash. That way he can't do nothing wrong that will land him in prison."

"I'm afraid that won't be so easy," the pastor says, and then pauses. He has observed several hundred Rosewood teenagers in these situations. He will do his best to shut off the supply lines to Marshall and his friends. But he knows that the young boys will find one if they want. This means that he must act quickly if Marshall does obtain a weapon. He will need Jay's help to find Marshall and convince him to give up the weapon before any harm results. He needs Jay to deliver the lines that best come from Dad: *I'm proud of you, son, and it can end here.*

Explaining all this to parents is never easy. Some feel, like Joycie, that the pastor wants youth to arm themselves. And, in some situations, ending a street conflict is easier when a young teen can show others just how far he is willing to go.

"It's going to be hard to stop him from buying one," the pastor continues. "We might be able to stop our friends on the street from selling him one. I'm working on that."

"I get it, Pastor," Jay says.

Jay then turns to his wife. "Joycie, Marshall's got to show he's a man. If he can put word on the streets that he's willing to shoot back, no one's gonna fear him again. So, we gotta let him get the gun. Then we can get it out of his hands."

"He ain't really fighting for his life," says Pastor Jesse. "He's fighting to be a *man*. He wants to make you proud of him—well, mostly your husband. He wants his dad to know he stood up for himself. Just like Dad did twenty years ago." The pastor winks at Jay. His due diligence had led him to uncover Jay's own brush with the criminal justice system and his own prison sentence for a violent act. The pastor sees a son wanting to walk in his father's footsteps.

Joycie looks at them in stunned silence. From her point of view, the proposed course of action is bizarre and unacceptable.

"We can get that gun out of his hands before he does something stupid," the pastor says. "But we really can't ever stop him from buying one. He won't get one around here—I can put the word out. But eventually, he and his friends will leave the community. They'll get one."

Jay calmly nods in agreement. Joycie says nothing.

"Good," says Pastor Jesse. "That means we're on the same page. Now pray with me. *That* we can always do."

31

While Pastor Jesse makes his rounds with parents, Officer Jerome is busy with his own intelligence gathering. He walks slowly through a flash thunderstorm on his way to Albert's church. He has worked with Antoine's uncle on family cases for years. He knows Albert's church so well that he now enters only via the back door—which is always unlocked. One should not be kept from a house of worship, so Uncle Albert reasons.

Jerome has set a goal for himself: he wants to establish the root of the story animating Frankie and Antoine: Why did Frankie attack? Why would a kid like Antoine keep sinking deeper into the morass of street life? The answers will get folded into the *officer's* story, which Jerome will deliver to Pastor Jesse. *This is how the situation looks from my perspective, and here's what we both can do.*

Jerome is careful to respect the investigating officers in his unit who are formally assigned to the case. He can't be seen as meddling. His unit already looks upon him as a combination of troublemaker and social worker. Neither role wins you friends among Chicago's cops. But Jerome knows the assigned officers need a quick win to please their commander. For a physical assault, cops typically show up for a few hours, ask a few questions, and head out. But a shooting means the assigned officers will need to demonstrate more resolve—and document more steps taken to ensure safety. Even though no one was hit by gunfire, community pressure will force the police to investigate how the guns ended up in the hands of the shooters, and whether the event is part of a more serious criminal operation. At the very least, the commander will communicate to church leaders, block club presidents, interested parents, and others that his team is actively looking into things.

Jerome knows the easiest win for the cops is to take a kid down to the station house for questioning. This helps them announce, "We did our best," and save face in the community. Jerome and Pastor Jesse would prefer that young boys avoid this fate if possible. Not only can the experience be traumatic, but the youth could be labeled as a snitch back on the streets, which places them in jeopardy. Better to restore calm informally.

Before Jerome reaches Albert's church, a few more text messages land on his phone. His source—a local homeless man—confirms that rival gang leaders are planning a violent takeover of Willie's crew as soon as midweek.

Jerome pokes his head through the church's back entrance. He shakes off the rain and walks in quietly. He is here to confirm some intel he received: Antoine will replace Frankie as the new crew chief. Jerome knows that the first few weeks are unstable times for newly appointed leaders. They might be scared, make bad decisions, or anger their bosses—all factors that can push them out of leadership as fast as they came in. For Jerome, this means there may still be time to pull Antoine out of that role.

From Missie and other sources, Jerome has enough information to question Antoine's decision to accept a leadership offer. He would understand if Antoine had joined a more accomplished gang to make a few bucks before heading to college. But letting his future ride on an association with Willie's hapless crew—one that is easy prey to armed rivals—doesn't make sense. Jerome reasons that there must be another reason, besides love of the gang life, that is motivating Antoine. This motivation could be his chance to intervene.

The bond between Albert and Jerome didn't take long to form. Their first meeting was in Holden Park years ago. Standing at the edge of the largest pond, at the southern edge, Jerome was pacifying a disturbed older man who held a knife to the throat of a twelve-year-old. The child was a brother of a local drug dealer. The kidnapper's motive: a large bag of dope from the drug dealer in exchange for the release of the child.

When Albert arrived and asked if he could be helpful, Jerome instructed him to stay back. The officer said, following the script, that the situation called for a more seasoned police negotiator. One was on his way.

Albert laughed and said the man would slit the young boy's throat in about ten minutes. He ignored Jerome's instructions and walked over with a Bible in his hand. A minute later, the man started weeping uncontrollably and handed over the knife to Albert.

Jerome ran and grabbed the young boy, Albert put his arms around the older man to pray, and the crowd went home.

Jerome's curiosity was piqued for many reasons—including that he had found a local who might work with him in neighborhood affairs. He asked what Albert said to the perp.

Albert responded, "I've seen this man before. I asked him, 'Why did God send the whale to swallow Jonah?' The man said what many say—that Jonah was a fool who didn't obey God. I told him, 'No! The fool was the one who threw Jonah into the ocean!' I had to explain that God sent this little boy to him for the same reason as the whale was sent to Jonah: because he so loves him. And this is the only way a proud man would ask for help. He asked if God had sent me. I said, 'Yes.'"

With that, Jerome and Albert begin meeting regularly. Theirs would become a private language—much like that between Jerome and Pastor Jesse—filled with archetype, myth, speculation. Their touchstone is the contemporary Sisyphus-like journey of young men and women pushing stones up ghetto hills. Any passerby to their discussion might feel they have landed in a college classroom. Or ancient Greece.

One of Jerome's favorite questions for Albert is "How far can you push a man before he explodes?" One of Albert's favorite retorts to kick off the discussion is "In what situations should you *allow* the man to explode?"

They are about to take up this very debate. The man in question is Antoine.

Albert's church is nearly empty. Three women congregate in the front with open Bibles. Jerome sits in the back, watching dripping rainwater make puddles on the unfinished concrete floor.

Albert walks over, removes his jacket, opens up his open Bible, and says a long prayer before the two men speak.

As Albert prays, Jerome considers the options for helping Antoine. Even though it might place him at risk, Jerome believes there are clear advantages if Antoine takes over command of Willie's crew — at least for a short period of time. Frankie would no longer be in charge — which means he would not make rash decisions that put others at risk. And Antoine could say to himself that he did everything possible to help his mother — making money illegally, even running a drug gang. Jerome wants to find Antoine quickly to remind him of this fact, and then encourage him to get out.

To determine whether this is viable, Jerome first needs to understand Antoine's background — why he joined and how much he wants to leave the crew. Albert is the best place to start.

After finishing the prayer, Albert launches immediately into the discussion about Antoine. Jerome can tell he hasn't slept much.

"You're thinking that I didn't do nothing about my nephew," Albert begins. "That I ignored Antoine, hoping things would get better by themselves. Well, Officer, in my line of work, the Lord doesn't wait long to tell you the first lesson of pastoral work. You can't make the bed when people are sleeping in it."

"Never heard that one." Jerome laughs. "What passage is that from?"

"From my grandfather — Grandpappy," Albert continues. "That man spent his whole life training people like me. Took me out for walks around the neighborhood. We'd stop at *this* man or *that* woman. They'd give us a tale of woe. Always something awful—lost their job, found out they were sick, about to die. Endless pains. Grandpappy would look over at me, even when they was standing there, and say, 'See this one over here. He's still sleeping in his bed, so nothing you can do. Ain't no point straightening out the sheets. Let's move on.' "

"You just leave people? You didn't even pray for them?" Jerome asks.

"You know something, Jerome. I asked Grandpappy that question on our first day together. He said, 'You ain't *leaving* them. No, sir! This is how you *join* them.' Never really understood it, but it made sense. Know what I mean?"

Jerome has little to say. He knows that Albert has avoided interfering in Antoine's life, so that his nephew can learn life lessons on his own. But just how far would Albert go? At what point would he say, "Enough is enough," and take Antoine out? Jerome knows that now is not the time for this discussion, so he stays silent.

"Officer, I'd like you to find Antoine," Albert says quietly.

"Why me? What can I do that you *can't* do?"

"See, when Antoine was twelve, my sister—*his* momma—got sick. She asked me not to tell Antoine that his momma would be gone in a few years. We left that part out. So we needed him to learn how to manage those feelings before that day came. We needed him to get used to taking care of her while she was ill. Make sense?"

"Yes, I get it. You needed him to practice feeling scared and anxious," Jerome interjects. "And I'm supposed to help him make better decisions when things get tough. Is that the plan?"

"Thank you," Albert acknowledges. "And, I do trust you, Jerome. You do what you need to do with Antoine." Albert rises up and says another soft prayer. He then pats Jerome on the back and heads over to greet another group of women who have come to pray.

Jerome is content. He has found Antoine's story—a young man needs to show his mother, the world, and himself just how far he is willing to go to be a good son. Jerome will need to speak with Antoine right away, reminding him that he has already stepped up like any honorable young man to help his mother.

To make this work, Jerome knows there is one other step involved. He will need to communicate with Willie that he cannot retaliate against either Antoine or Frankie for leaving the gang. Will the incarcerated drug boss listen? Jerome isn't certain, but like Albert, he doesn't see another way out.

32

Harpoon is back at Sweetwater, his local corner bar. All day, he will attend to team matters from this seat. Via text, he will approve new customers, suggest negotiation tactics on sales inquiries, and ask for intel on prospective customers.

Pastor Jesse pulls up a seat and joins him at his table. The lunchtime crowd filters in. Ribs and greens is the special of the day. Most grab and go, but Harpoon and the Pastor eat at a small table with two freshly poured glasses of milk.

Usually the pastor calls Harpoon for a favor. Today, it is Harpoon who requested the meetup. He has some bigger issues on his mind.

Pastor Jesse watches as Harpoon's eyes turn glassy and moist. "It always feels better after you tell someone," Pastor Jesse starts off slowly. "Whatever it is can't be that bad."

Harpoon takes a sip from his straw and takes off his cream-colored Chicago White Sox cap.

"I got to think about what's next, Pastor," Harpoon says. "Let me just leave it at that."

"I see," Pastor Jesse responds. "How long you been thinking about this, can I ask?"

"About three or four months."

Pastor Jesse smiles to himself. Based on this response he feels certain that Harpoon either wants to run a legitimate business—which means needing to launder his money—or he is about to be a father. Or both.

"You tell me when you're ready," Pastor Jesse says quietly.

"You know Teresa's daughter, right? Cherise? Family used to go to your church a while back."

"Yes, I do," the pastor responds. "The daddy—Lucius—died last year. Ain't seen them both since the services."

"Well," Harpoon says. "There's something I need to talk to you about. Me and Cherise."

"I have an opportunity for you," Pastor Jesse smiles, knowing he has guessed correctly. "I can get you out and I'll get all your ladies out too. Every one of them. They will be working. No one will ever sell a gun again—I'll see to it that none of you go back to that world. If it makes sense, you let me know. But first, how you feeling about being a daddy? Scary, ain't it?"

Harpoon's shoulders relax. He tries to answer the question, but he is too emotional to speak.

"That's okay," Pastor Jesse says. "We ain't in no rush. While you think on it, let me tell you how scared I was. Man, I'll never forget the day I found out I would bring a child into this world."

33

News of Pastor Jesse's intervention has spread around the neighborhood. No one will risk a firearms sale to Marshall's group. Every effort by Marshall, Georgie, and Siron to reach a local gun seller—pro or amateur—fails. It is Georgie who then broadcasts across social media the group's need of a weapon. He posts messages on Facebook and Twitter to attract the attention of gun sellers. Unfamiliar with this approach, he makes little effort to disguise his request.

> *Who gonna give us what we need? We coming out shooting at some niggers!*

He makes sure to announce that the group is on the hunt for *payback*. There is no mistaking the subtext: he will pay top dollar for a firearm.

There is also no mistaking the responses he receives. Text after text, tweet after tweet, makes it clear that the boys will be hard-pressed to find a gun in Rosewood.

You all are too hot!
Cops watching, nigger. Stay low.

A message soon arrives from Georgie's cousin Cleet that opens up a new window of opportunity.

G. Don't be no fool. 2 many eyes on you. Come see me.

Cleet, who lives a few hundred miles away in Decatur, has come to their aid by scouring various social media channels for cheap weapons sales outside of Chicago. He deep dives on Facebook and Instagram, common channels for gun trafficking. There are sellers offloading old guns, worn and busted up. Some display the goods proudly as showpieces from infamous street gangs—88th Street CVL, State Street Gangster Disciples. A burgeoning souvenir trade, black-market style. And, for Marshall and Georgie, it is turning out to be a more reasonable marketplace.

Cleet proves to be an effective middleman. He locates six viable candidates, all within a fifty-mile radius of his home. Marshall, Georgie, and the others take quick action. This time, their efforts to fundraise prove more successful. They pool together a few hundred bucks, which includes loans from empathetic cousins and friends, that they promise to pay back.

Marshall and his friends welcome this positive sign. The aftermath of the ambush is not only tense but embarrassing. Their peers have been playing up their impotence on social media.

Look at those pussies! Too fucking scared to come out
and fight!
Frankie 1. Bitches 0.
Come to school and get your ass whupping #2!

Their shame is growing by the day.

Georgie and Siron call for a midnight meeting of the full team.
Each boy sneaks out of the house and runs over to the brownstone.
Georgie reports the news from cousin Cleet. He volunteers to drive
to Decatur. Marshall puts up little resistance. He says he will join
Georgie on the trip. Siron and the others agree to break out of their
house and spy on Frankie's crew.

This leaves the only other major decision: When would they go
after Frankie—and how?

Georgie is in control. "We can't sit around too long," he warns.
"Those niggers gonna find out we left town—they know we came
back with something. So, we got to go fast once we get something."

"He's right," Siron affirms. "As soon as you all return, we do it.
But no one say nothing stupid. No one fuck this up."

"Ain't that gonna look kind of funny?" Marshall asks. "If all of
a sudden, none of us say nothing on Facebook?"

"Don't care," replies Siron. "We got to surprise them niggers
when we roll up on them."

34

On Saturday morning, Marshall walks out of his bedroom and into the kitchen for a drink and a snack.

"Hello, Marshall," an unfamiliar voice welcomes him. It is Pastor Jesse. He is seated at the dining room table alongside Marshall's parents. The air is heavy and the mood is solemn. Marshall can tell they are in the middle of prayers. "Come, sit and join us."

The pastor holds the largest of the seventeen Bibles in the Mariot household. Grandma keeps this particular black book in the kitchen. It is heavy, worn, and filled with the family's years of gratitude and searching. Lying beside the Bible is a small black chair her own father built. On this chair Marshall's grandmother read the morning prayer — at least that was her routine until sickness forced her to a bed and to a more modest book of psalms.

The Mariot family tradition is a simple one: if anyone reads a passage, then everyone must read. No one may refuse. Pastor Jesse is intent on upholding this tradition. Marshall sits in the corner with a Mountain Dew in his hand, while the pastor selects a small teaching on sin and redemption.

"God always speaks to the man about to fall from grace," the pastor says. "Only question is whether that man is listening." His eyes never leave Marshall as he speaks about the plight of a man about to do wrong.

Then comes a few more prayers, some light banter, and then Pastor Jesse turns to Marshall.

"No one said it would be easy—what you're going through," he says, squeezing in a smile to offset the serious tone. "But, we were all young, just like you. And we get it."

Joycie shoots Marshall a stare, urging him to respond.

"Yes, sir," Marshall says. Marshall doesn't like all the attention focused on him. He shifts his gaze downward, in hopes that everyone will walk out of the room and leave him alone.

"You're going to be seeing me more often, son," Pastor Jesse says, as he takes both Jay and Joycie by the hand. "I know it ain't no fun being your age and being *watched*." The pastor places an extra emphasis on the constant surveillance that Marshall has discovered to be a part of his life.

"Yes, sir," Marshall says, his eyes staying fixed on the floor.

Pastor Jesse puts on his hat, tips it gently, and bows his head. "Expecting to see all of you tomorrow," he remarks, and walks out of the house.

35

Harpoon is standing on a street, two hundred miles south of Chicago, taking in the scenery of his childhood. He and Missie have traveled downstate to pick up several dozen used weapons from some rural farmhands. He sips on his tea and stares at familiar streets.

A few years ago, Harpoon's family began leaving central Illinois for small towns throughout the Midwest and South. Today, the small farms, trailer parks, and clusters of single-family dwellings where he grew up are a pickup location for his team's quarterly bulk weapons buys. The region is a favorite stopping point for Harpoon to reminisce, especially on a brisk autumn day, like today, when the swirling dust and the morning dew brings out the familiar scent of his youth.

Harpoon has brought Missie downstate for a sizable gun buy. He has purchased fifteen used handguns from a rural family that has gathered up the cache from neighbors. Then, it is on to a trailer park, where another local broker has gathered up twelve used guns from friends and neighbors. Harpoon and Missie will get in and out quickly and head back to Chicago with the cache.

He is also there for a conversation with Missie. Harpoon will let her know of his plans to exit the gun trade. If she wishes, she can take over the business.

For the drive downstate, Missie has agreed to be play the roles of both driver and security. This means she will be responsible for the directions and for standing guard while Harpoon executes the trades. In the last year, Missie has chosen to avoid these trips. The work in Chicago keeps her busy and she prefers to send another team member and hire part-time residents to provide security for Harpoon. But Harpoon insisted she join him on this venture.

Farther down the street, in front of a single-story light-blue cottage that serves as the entrance to a small residential enclave, a wind-blown placard leans eastward, fighting the wind: House for Sale.

Harpoon gets back in the car. "I got something I need to show you," he tells Missie. "We got to make a quick stop."

They drive up to the blue cottage and park across the street. Harpoon gets out and leans against the side door. Harpoon does not have to talk very long before Missie predicts the motivation for their conversation. Harpoon stammers, unable to tell her in a clear, simple way why he wants to exit the gun trade.

"You gonna be a daddy, ain't you?" She laughs. She has been thinking as much for the better part of a month. "You and Cherise gonna start a family. I'm happy for you. Don't know why you couldn't just tell me."

Harpoon is grateful for Missie's observation. His shoulders relax and he lets out a deep breath.

"Don't tell me you thinking of leaving Chicago?!" Missie laughs. "You want to live . . . *here*?!" She stares at the small blue cottage with the FOR SALE sign blowing in the wind.

Harpoon does not answer. He doesn't need to.

They talk for a few more minutes—about the only other topic worth discussing: Would Missie be willing to take over the entire operation?

Harpoon goes over details. He wants to stay involved, but at a distance. "It's yours. I'll help out—find your shit when you come down here to visit, help you if you get in trouble. But, I'm out, Missie. You gonna be running things. I ain't gonna get in your way."

Missie is silent. She is fidgety. She lights a cigarette and looks around.

"I want to keep it in the family," Harpoon says. "You're family to me."

"I don't know," Missie say. "I ain't so young anymore. I want a family myself."

"I kinda figured you did," Harpoon says. There is no point pushing her any further. Either she is willing to run the crew after Harpoon exits, or he will have to dissolve the business.

"Just think on it," Harpoon says to Missie, not wanting to place too much pressure on her. "That's all I'm asking. You spent a long time building this up. Even if you want to get out, maybe do it after you get a little more cash in your pocket."

"*Mm-hmm,*" Missie says dreamily.

They both take a final look at the cottage and drive off.

36

The pastor is in his car, at the northern border of Holden Park, near his favorite duck pond. In his hand, a notepad logs his daily tasks. A half-dozen names appear in scribbles, each a young boy whose life has been upended. He looks through his notes and tries to plan a route from family to family that will let him meet with everyone before the night is over.

In the distance, the broken muffler of a blue Ford Taurus announces Calvin's approach. Willie has blessed Pastor Jesse's meeting with Calvin.

Earlier that morning, Pastor Jesse added another task to his list: understand Willie's motivation. He knows Willie can be a disruptive force, even when locked up. The drug boss could undermine the delicate truce the pastor is bringing together. Like everyone else, the pastor must rely on Calvin, who has just visited with Willie in prison, for insight into what Willie is thinking.

Today, the pastor has brought with him some of his own intel. He already knows that Willie's efforts to arm Frankie's team are being stymied. Gun sellers are rebuffing. *Shit is too hot on the streets*. Without guns, Willie's business will be in jeopardy. His unarmed crew will be too vulnerable, and customers and suppliers will abandon him. Willie should cooperate with the pastor, if only so he can keep hold of his prized sales spot. That's the pastor's strategy.

The driver's side of the car creaks open and Calvin struggles to lift himself out of the car. He breathes heavily as he drops next to the pastor. His shiny white Nike tracksuit squeaks as he settles into the pastor's black leather seats. He tries to speak, but the pastor puts a hand up and interrupts him. "Calvin, I've known Willie a long time. Never had no trouble with the man. But, I am not putting the lives of these young boys in jeopardy. Frankie should be chasing girls. He has no business selling that crap. That boy gonna get killed and his death gonna be on Willie."

Calvin takes a deep breath. "Yes, sir. Ain't nobody arguing with you, Pastor. Willie says he gonna take Frankie out for a while."

"I see," Pastor Jesse responds. He can tell this is only half the story. "Good for Frankie, I suppose. But what then?"

"He got someone else who gonna take over," Calvin says. "Frankie did some stupid shit by himself. Willie wants to make things right."

Pastor Jesse keeps pushing Calvin. "You telling me a teenage boy who never ran nothing is putting out a hit on another boy who never *sold* nothing or *hurt* nobody? Calvin, who you think you talking to?!" The pastor smirks.

Calvin shakes his head. "Pastor, I'm just supposed to pass what Willie tells me, okay? Willie just wants to get back to business."

"So, what next?"

Calvin pushes out the request hurriedly. "Willie needs to be protected. You know what he's like. He just can't be out there *un-protected*." Calvin stammers. His sentences don't connect well with one another. But he ends up making the point loud and clear to the pastor: Willie needs to buy firearms quickly or competitors will take over his group.

"Calvin, you go back to Willie and tell him I can't do that. I ain't here to help his business."

"Yeah, Willie and I both figured you'd say something like that."

Pastor Jesse stews. Willie has placed him in a difficult situation. The drug boss will use his thug-free status not just to increase drug sales but to obtain as many weapons as possible. This would reduce the likelihood of a takeover, and therefore potential violence from a gang fight.

There must be another way besides giving Willie what he wants, Pastor Jesse thinks to himself. Such is the dilemma of the *bubble*. Even street traders, gang members, and drug traffickers prefer calm since it is good for their business.

The pastor doesn't like his options.

"I got to get outta here," the pastor shouts at Calvin. "And, don't say nothing to Willie until I call you later tonight. You got that? And pray with me." Calvin bows his head. Pastor Jesse sends a quick text message to Jerome. Then, closing his eyes, he selects a passage from his morning prayer. "Gentle Shepherd, we come to You as we are, not as we pretend to be."

37

On Sunday, Marshall sits in a car with Georgie and Jacquez far out in the Illinois countryside. The sheets of rain splattering
the windshield and the steady *whoosh* of the car heater fill their ears.
Marshall can feel doubt not-so-gently knocking on the door and
testing him. *Should i get out of here before I get in trouble? What if I
get killed buying the gun? What if cops put me in Cook County Jail
and I get beat?* On it goes, the mental back and forth. As Marshall
grows more weary, it becomes harder to quiet down these voices.

Georgie's cousin, Cleet, has instructed them to drive to a re-
mote trailer park. The path through the farmlands is a labyrinth of
windy roads, nestled in stretches of forest and interrupted by small,
harvested plots. Old vehicles of all types sit abandoned in fields
and ditches.

Marshall's car has pulled up outside a family trailer that is set off
in two acres of woods, along with a dozen other mobile homes and
vans. Marshall spots a group of white and Black teens taking cover
under a sagging, brown side awning, next to a barbecue and fire pit.

Two large dogs drag themselves to greet the newcomers, more out of obligation than genuine curiosity. Behind them, Cleet walks up in a soaked black hoodie and dumps himself inside the back seat.

Georgie's cousin is businesslike and abrupt. "Georgie, c'mon, get the cash and come over."

Marshall hands over the roll of bills and sinks back into the seat. Through the dirtied window, he sees one of the white teens pulling back a blue plastic tarp.

A few minutes of haggling is all it takes for Georgie and Cleet to run back to the car.

"Three hundred and fifty ain't gonna do it," Georgie says, surprising Marshall with the sudden change in price. "They now want four hundred and twenty-five for both."

"I don't have any more money," Marshall says. "What we gonna do? Why can't we buy just one?"

"White boy say you got to buy *two*," Cleet speaks up. "Can't someone send you money?"

"Lanea," Georgie says. "Call your sister, Marshall. Do it now."

Marshall groans. He snuck out of the house to make the trip. If he calls Lanea, asking for the money, she will tell Dad he is probably looking for a weapon.

"I don't know," Marshall says, shaking his head. "I don't know." His voice trails off.

"We ain't really got time, Marshall. You got to do it now. We ain't gonna find two Glocks for this price back home. Lanea is our best shot. You got to ask her right now. Get on the phone." Georgie and his cousin jump out of the car and run back over to buy some time.

Marshall knows Georgie is right. This rural Illinois sale may be their only option. They lost their connection to Jonny Isaac after the Friday night attack. And no one else in Rosewood will sell them a gun. All week, their queries to street hustlers in the community have brought forth the same response: *We can't sell you nothing, because the cops will come down heavy on us.*

Marshall sends a text to Lanea. He decides not to ask her for money. Instead, he tells her he is with Georgie and asks her to meet him later that afternoon. He needs to speak with her before the group goes after Frankie and his crew. He could use her advice.

———

Tap, tap, tap!

The sound on the car window startles Marshall. Georgie stares at him with a grin stretching from ear to her. He holds up a paper bag and pushes it against the car window for Marshall to see.

"We got it!" Georgie shouts, his teeth chattering from the cold. "We got it."

Georgie plops into the seat. "Jacquez, wake up. Let's get out of here!" His shoulders lower and he lets out a sigh. No words are necessary. Marshall knows exactly what Georgie is trying to say: *All the trouble we took to come downstate is worth it. We finally got a gun!*

Marshall watches Georgie slowly pull out a used Browning handgun. Georgie grabs the frayed brown grip, lifts the barrel up, and points the muzzle straight through the windshield. It is duller and less attractive than the brilliant Magnum that Jonny first showed them more than a week ago. And it is slightly bigger than the handgun that Jonny fired during the Friday night attack. Georgie looks over the gun, as though scanning for a secret button. After a few seconds, he turns it around and points it at Marshall.

"Don't point that thing at me!" Marshall says, refusing to take hold of the pistol. "I'll look at it later. And don't we need more money?"

"We have to pay Cleet back." Georgie responds. "I promised we would do that."

"How we gonna *do* that?!" Marshall asks.

"Hell, I don't know, maybe we steal it from Frankie's boys when go after them," Georgie smiles. "We only need one anyway. Cleet said he would take the other one if we can't find the money."

As Jacquez pulls away, Marshall asks, "How long we got to hide it before we go after them? I told you I can't keep it in my house."

Georgie ignores the question. "Everyone's waiting for us. We got to stay with our plan. Tomorrow. We gonna do it tomorrow. We gonna make Frankie understand we ain't fucking around. So don't plan to go nowhere, Marshall. We need you there."

"Maybe we should wait a little longer?" Marshall suggests. "Maybe we should get everyone together and talk."

"Don't need to," Georgie says. "Siron texted. He said Frankie's boys have been outside every night. Said we may even just do it tonight when we get back. Just get it over with."

"Don't we need to get ready for this?!" Marshall raises his voice. He presumed the group would make a more elaborate plan back on the stoop. Racing over to Frankie's doesn't seem wise.

It dawns on Marshall that he is not the leader of the group. What started out as his problem is now a *group* beef. And Georgie and Siron are in charge. Marshall dismisses the thought. He never really wanted to be the leader, he tells himself. He just wanted a group by his side—one that would come to his defense.

Marshall looks at his phone. He hopes that Georgie will not ask the group to drive to Frankie's before he can speak with his sister. He closes his eyes. He wishes he could phone his dad. He wishes he could reach into the sky to hold his grandpa's hand.

A small part of him badly wants to reveal everything to Dad. He wants to be stopped before it is too late. He always thought of the gun as a deterrent. It was just something to scare away Frankie and his crew. But now, with the weapon in the front seat, everything feels too real. He no longer feels in control.

Jacquez moves through the last part of the winding road and into the straightaway that leads to the highway on-ramp. The car accelerates past barren fields and modest tract houses. Georgie turns the heater on full blast and turns the radio even louder. The local rap station is playing a Common and Kanye duet:

> *I walked in the crib, got two kids*
> *And my baby momma late (uh oh, uh oh, uh oh)*

Marshall puts his head back and closes his eyes. It is at least a three hour ride back to Rosewood. He might as well take a nap. On most Sundays, he looks forward to their family routine: he and his sister act surprised when Dad announces, "Let's go eat at McDonald's!" Dad doesn't care if they fake their surprise. Everyone laughs at the silly ritual and looks forward to pancakes, Big Macs, fries, and strawberry shakes.

Marshall begins to dream up an excuse for his absence. He knows he will need a good one when he walks in the door.

38

On Sunday morning, Jay, Joycie, and Lanea wake to find Marshall is out of the house. They promised Pastor Jesse that the family would attend services at his church.

"He went over to Georgie's," Lanea tells them, in an effort to provide some cover for Marshall. "Said he needed to get out of the house. He says he'll be back tonight."

Jay and Joycie say little. Marshall sometimes will miss church, preferring to hang out with his friends. Typically, Jay will tell Joycie it is normal for a teenager to miss church, and Joycie will accept his explanation begrudgingly. Today feels different. Jay comforts her with a few words: "It's okay, don't worry." But he knows Marshall is likely scheming with his friends. And given that Marshall is still under a curfew, Jay concludes the scheme must be serious.

After church services, they exit with the other parishioners, queuing up to shake the hands of the gospel choir who bid everyone goodbye.

Pastor Jesse approaches and pulls Jay aside. Jay mentions that

Marshall is out with his friends. This time, Jay is the one receiving comfort from the pastor. "He's a good kid, you have to trust him right now. He's going to do what he feels is necessary."

Then Pastor Jesse shares some unexpected news. "That boy Frankie. He's disappeared," Pastor Jesse says, his face expressionless. "We think he ran away because he felt he was in danger. Probably just hiding somewhere."

"If Frankie's gone, then Marshall doesn't need to fight anymore," Jay says out loud, thinking to himself and following the pastor's lead. "It's over."

Pastor Jesse laughs. "Over? Maybe. Marshall will feel he never showed you he was a man. That's what this is about. And his friends may go through with whatever they are planning. They may pressure him."

Jay doesn't say anything. Pastor Jesse can see that Jay feels unsure. The wind picks up. The sound from a car stereo gets louder and the pastor takes a step closer.

"The Lord is calling you, Jay. You're being asked to be there for your son. You need to convince him a man can walk away. Sometimes that means walking away from his friends. Can you do that?"

Jay nods, shakes the Pastor's hand, and walks away.

39

Late Sunday afternoon, Marshall, Georgie, and Jacquez finish their drive home from downstate Illinois. Their journey was a success. When they go after Frankie's crew, they will be armed.

But it is too late to head over to Frankie's spot, so Marshall and Georgie decide they will stay inside at Georgie's house. Georgie sends a text to their friends to meet at the brownstone the following morning, 8:00 a.m. Georgie is too nervous to bring a weapon inside, even if it is well concealed. He and Marshall hide their newly purchased weapon in a paper bag underneath a bush in Georgie's backyard. Georgie grabs a sleeping bag for Marshall, and they quietly head into the bedroom.

Marshall texts Lanea, who lets her parents know that Marshall is staying over at Georgie's house. They both know their mom will call Georgie's parents to make sure he is there. For good measure, Marshall texts his dad to say he'll be back home after school tomorrow.

Marshall's sleep is fitful. He wakes up on the floor and texts Lanea, asking his sister to meet him on her way to school. He wants one final conversation with her before going after Frankie's crew. Without waking Georgie, he sneaks out of the house.

A bleached-white morning sun beds down over the row of trees at the eastern border of Holden Park. The shadow over Marshall's feet recedes slowly as a soft light brings the frost up from the grass. A few hundred feet away, the last summer growths in a small community garden stretch a few inches up to the sky.

Waves of wind sail through Marshall's down jacket. Shivering, he walks around the brownstone stoop to stay warm. The butt of the handgun tucked into his underwear presses against his skin.

Lanea is walking briskly across the park toward Marshall. She starts their conversation twenty yards before reaching him.

"You know Frankie's gone, right? No one knows where he is," Lanea says. "You should just forget about him."

Marshall smirks. He refuses her advice. He needs to finish what he began, which means going after the entire crew that attacked him. "*We* need to take care of business. And we gonna do it."

Lanea pauses. She can see through Marshall. He wants help, but he is being stubborn. "Dad gets it, Marshall," she says. "Dad knows what you need to do. I told you to call him."

Marshall shakes his head.

"What you want to talk about, then?" Lanea asks.

Marshall shrugs his shoulders. "Don't know. Just got to do what I got to do."

Lanea stares at him, frustrated that her advice is being ignored. She starts walking away, with a funny feeling that Marshall is hiding something serious from her. She decides to send a text message to Dad. This would be a good time for Dad to find Marshall, she reasons, before he does something he will regret. Dad might be able to calm him down and convince him to let go of his feud with Frankie's crew.

Marshall *wants* to call his father. But he feels too embarrassed. What if Dad views him as a failure because he called for help? Even if Frankie has left town, he decides he needs to avenge his honor and go after the entire crew—whoever is still around. Then, and only then, will he report to his father.

As Lanea's figure recedes into the distance, Marshall turns and sprints off, heading across the park toward Frankie's home base.

Halfway into the park, he takes cover behind a clump of overgrown brush. He is a hundred yards away from the crew's house. He should be with Georgie and his team, but he feels compelled to act on his own. It started as his battle and he wants to finish it this way. He will not make it to the morning meeting at the brownstone.

It is a big risk to go forward alone. There is the chance that Frankie's crew will spot him and come after him. If they see he has a weapon, they might shoot at him. These thoughts come and go. What stays with him is the chance to win back his honor. No one expects him to actually defeat a much older, experienced drug crew. But if he acts—and acts alone—they can no longer mistake his courage.

The scene plays out in his head—standing on Frankie's turf, a weapon in his hand, defending himself while Frankie's crew retreats. But, as Marshall contemplates practical matters, his conviction weakens. He thinks of Georgie and the rest of his friends. They will certainly be upset at his sudden change of tactics. They have their own manhood to defend. *Why didn't you wait for us?* they will ask him. He will risk the loss of their friendship if he acts alone.

With these thoughts bouncing in his head, Marshall's breath quickens. The second-guessing is giving him a headache. Georgie and the rest of the team are probably on their way to the brownstone.

40

Across the park, Pastor Jesse waits in front of Marshall's grandpa's brownstone. He is there to speak with Marshall and his friends. This is part of the plan that he and Officer Jerome came up with the night before based on two pieces of information: Frankie is no longer managing Willie's crew and, as Jay told the pastor, Marshall had been with Georgie all of Sunday without coming home. "They're up to something," Jay said, and the pastor agreed. These details are enough for the two to guess that Marshall's friends may be planning a quick retaliation and they could possess a weapon.

Hearing from Jay that the group meets at the brownstone, Pastor Jesse drives over to speak with the boys before they reach school. Perhaps he can persuade the teens that they can walk away and hold their heads high. More than likely, if he is successful, they will start boasting on social media that they scared Frankie away.

Pastor Jesse pulls up to the brownstone, finds no one there, and decides to wait. He sits in his car, switching channels on the

AM radio. He stops at a Christian station where an old friend, a fellow pastor from the seminary, delivers the daily sermon. A gospel tune follows and the pastor shuts his eyes. Late last night, he visited a hospital room on Chicago's far South Side because the evening sent him a local teen who was the victim of gun violence. Another family needing to be soothed, another young boy whose name would appear in the pastor's Book of Names.

The chatter of boys running past the car wakes the pastor abruptly. Marshall's friends stream down the sidewalk and lurch their way up the stairs to the brownstone stoop. The group settles in, pulling out phones and typing furiously. Pastor Jesse rubs his eyes, says a small prayer, pulls up his socks, and tightens the laces on his black wing-tip shoes. Taking a full breath, he opens the door and walks toward the group.

"Do you know who I am?" Pastor Jesse says, adjusting his hat and taking a seat on the cold stone stoop next to Georgie.

The boys place their heads down and lower their voices. The pastor needs no introduction.

"I'll take that as an invitation to speak," Pastor Jesse says. "I know you're waiting for Marshall."

"He'll be here," Siron says. His voice quivers as he tries to show some resolve. "He's with us."

"He's not going to let us down," Georgie follows up.

Pastor Jesse smiles. The boys are scared.

"Well, you're right about that. And I'm going to sit here with you," Pastor Jesse says. "I got nowhere I need to be. So, if he comes, we can all talk. If he doesn't, then I want you to consider something. Today, I'm watching you. Tomorrow, my friend, Officer Jerome, will be here. Then we'll get your teacher to come around. After that,

Mr. Wilson, who runs the Boys and Girls Club, will give you the *eye*. Is that what you want?"

Silence.

"See, we're watching you now because we know you did nothing wrong. If you and Marshall do what you're planning to do, we'll be watching because we can't trust you to take care of yourself. That's not the kind of *watching* you want. Either way, we love you! But you don't want us to be looking at you all the time. Not like that. Know what I mean?"

The thought of being watched night and day is the least desirable situation for any young teenager. No one speaks.

"Maybe you'd like to pray with me?" Pastor Jesse says, picking up his Bible. "After that, I think I'll leave you all to talk amongst yourselves. You know where the church is. You know where to find me. And I hope you'll go on your way after I leave. Know you are all loved. Very much."

Through two short prayers, the boys bow their heads down respectfully and say nothing. The pastor makes his way slowly down to the car.

Georgie follows him. "Marshall was supposed to be here, but he's late," he tells Pastor Jesse. The pastor can tell that Georgie is surprised by Marshall's absence. And a little concerned.

"Anything else you want to say to me, young man?" the pastor asks. He knows it won't take long for Georgie to tell him what is really going on.

Georgie, eyes lowered and solemn, says nothing.

"Did you also go with him to get that weapon?" The pastor takes a guess that they found a weapon—it is the only way he can explain the fact they spent the entire day and night together.

Georgie is visibly ashamed. Like the pastor can see right through him.

Pastor Jesse can tell he has guessed correctly. "That's what I'm most concerned about right now. You seem smart enough to understand why."

"I don't have it. Not right now, anyway," Georgie says, lifting his eyes for a moment. "I looked for it this morning, but . . ."

Pastor Jesse has all the information he needs. "You have one more thing you need to do for me. Tell everyone to go home and stay home. Not to school, not back here. You got that?"

Georgie nods, letting out a meek "Yes, sir," and heads back to the stoop.

Although the entire circle of friends is involved in the dispute with Frankie's crew, Pastor Jesse knows it is best to focus his efforts on Marshall. It is Marshall who is working the hardest to save face. If they can find Marshall and enable him to walk away with his head high, his friends will be uplifted.

The pastor calls Jerome and they quickly discuss next steps. If they find Marshall—and he has a weapon—Jerome will bring Marshall to the police station. There, they will speak with the officers assigned to investigating the Friday night melee. The officers are not interested in Marshall, since he was a passive victim. But the formal questioning will scare Marshall and his friends. And it should enable Marshall to broadcast widely that it was the police who stopped him, not his fear.

If he finds a gun on Marshall, Jerome will turn in the weapon to the officers. "Marshall did the right thing and turned in the weapon," Jerome will say. There is little guarantee that the officers will give Marshall the benefit of the doubt. They may not drop the weapons possession charges. For this to happen, Jerome knows he must appeal to their desire to spend their time addressing more serious crimes.

Once Marshall has been taken into the station, word will spread. And the pastor could visit Georgie and the others to tell them what's happening. Marshall's friends are not seasoned gang members for whom police attention might give them greater status. The news that the cops are watching should make the rest of the group reluctant to move forward.

Neither of these two tasks mark the end of the intervention. But getting the gun out of Marshall's hands and scaring the group will give the two men more time to keep their diplomacy moving forward.

Pastor Jesse sends a text message to Marshall's father—Please call me. He might need some help convincing Marshall to relinquish the weapon. Jay's presence might be enough to convince a scared and overheated young man to head down to the police station.

A few minutes later, the phone rings and Pastor Jesse answers the call from Jay.

"Nothing good can happen if we don't find your son right away," he says. "At least before Jerome's friends find him and take him in."

"Maybe I could drive him?" Jay asks.

"Yes. I have a good feeling," the pastor nods. "It will be fine."

Pastor Jesse has already imagined worst case scenarios. The chance that Marshall will walk up and fire indiscriminately upon the crew is low. More likely, Marshall will shoot from afar or just up in the air. But both actions could place a wider group of bystanders at risk.

Finding Marshall before this occurs is not the only challenge. The pastor must ensure that other police officers do not locate Marshall first. If they find a gun, they will view Marshall as a serious public threat. For his plan to work, Pastor Jesse must get to Marshall first and take the gun out of Marshall's hands.

41

Members of the crew, which is now led by Antoine, pull into the driveway to set up their daily operations. Keeping himself hidden, Marshall sits across the street, watching the team go through their motions. A tall crew member in a blue tracksuit pulls an aging light-blue Chevy minivan across the driveway, blocking anyone from making their way up to the house. He grabs a few folding chairs from the back and places them next to the sidewalk. Another crew member takes a seat, facing the street. A third, wearing a pair of dark metal sunglasses, stands on the porch of the house, scanning the crowd. The customers line up, ignoring the instructions that they not loiter. Cars come up slowly and the team waves them off as well.

Then someone whistles loudly from the window of the house behind them. The store is officially open.

There is motion. The teen on the chair waves the cars to go around the block so they can queue up properly. He signals for the walk-up buyers to form an orderly line. Another one walks over and takes their cash. After stuffing the cash in his jacket pocket, he sends them to the side of the house to pick up their drugs.

Marshall's eyes are fixed on the street ballet. So much commotion, yet everything seems to fall in place. The customers arrive sometimes alone, sometimes in small groups. Every so often, their laughter is interrupted by the fraying muffler of a passing car. No one appears concerned about hiding the activity or keeping a low profile. Passersby ignore the commotion, looking past as though it were a high school car wash. There is not a police officer to be seen.

Marshall can feel himself inching forward. He feels dizzy and unsure. He considers running up to the crew and enacting his revenge. *But what do I do when I get there?* Should he shoot at someone or simply shout a warning? What will the girls at school and everybody online consider a successful retaliation? Does he need to fire the weapon or just wave it around?

Marshall stares at the house, and a vibrant, humming sales team is giving him a sinking feeling. There is little good that will come out of being here. Not only is he outnumbered but he is not as experienced as Frankie's crew in any form of street conflict—with or without weapons.

Marshall needs more time. And more cover. He walks back fifty yards to a small bench, tucked behind a fence at the edge of the softball field. His phone buzzes. It is his father: Call me, now. Before replying, Marshall checks over the nearly dozen messages that he has sent to his friends. Still no response from Georgie, Siron, and the others. *Why are they ignoring me?* A part of him wants to return to the brownstone and start the morning over.

More texts from his father arrive. They are coming two at a

time. Dad is not known for being patient. He will repeatedly dial Marshall's number until he picks up—a tactic he has used quite successfully in the past when Marshall ignores him.

Marshall must make a decision. Either his father will find him soon or someone else will. He remembers why he came out to Frankie's alone. His pride. He is there to put an end to the local gossip—that he is scared, a *bitch*, a *pussy*. The words he has been reading online dig at him. *Any* action will be helpful, he concludes, to correct this perception.

His phone buzzes. Another text from his father. I know you seeing this, Marshall.

Marshall feels for the weapon that is now tucked into his inside jacket pocket. It no longer brings him the comfort he sought. He is paralyzed and unable to move. He wishes that someone would tell him what to do next.

Across the park, Marshall spots two men walk briskly down the path. He looks around. There is no one else near. He ignores the pair until they are about fifty yards away.

As the men near, Marshall gathers himself. He looks for a path back across the ball fields, away from the men and over to his grandpa's brownstone.

"Marshall, hold on a minute!" Pastor Jesse shouts.

Officer Jerome and Pastor Jesse take a position on either side of him.

Pastor Jesse checks the back of Marshall's pants for any bulges that might suggest the presence of a weapon. "Marshall, you want to give me your jacket? This is Officer Jerome. He's going to ask you a few questions."

Marshall is confused but turns over his jacket. Pastor Jesse feels around, stops when his hands discover the handgun, and then nods affirmatively to Jerome.

"Marshall, you're going to take a little trip with us. Okay? Some of my friends are going to ask you a few questions. Your dad will be here in a minute to take you. Sounds good?"

A few minutes later, Jay Mariot walks up, panting from rushing across the fields to see his son. He does his best to smile. Marshall can see his eyes are moist and that he is concerned. Jay puts his arm around his son.

"Marshall, let me tell you what I see," Pastor Jesse says, looking directly at the young man, who is shivering from being out in the park so long. "I see a proud young man wanting to defend himself and show the world that he ain't gonna take it no more. That's what I see. What about you, Officer Jerome?"

"Takes a lot of courage to get this far, Marshall, and not back down. But we do have a situation that needs to be addressed. And we're going to take you down to the police station."

Marshall looks surprised. *I never used the gun*, he thinks to himself. *Why am I in trouble?* He looks over at his dad, who pulls him in closer.

Jay hugs him and says nothing. Marshall not only was caught with a weapon, but in the middle of a planned effort to use it. A cop wouldn't need much more to press charges and introduce Marshall formally to the juvenile justice world. A juvenile's criminal record can be erased, but the stigma and shame, the feeling of failure, can haunt a teen for a long time. This was Jay's experience two decades ago, upon his first arrest. He survived because other adults came to his aid. Jay knows he will now need to be more vigilant—a more active force in Marshall's life. He hopes such a move, and some leniency from Jerome and the investigating officers, is enough to help Marshall stay *ordinary*.

Marshall walks back to the parking lot with three adults following behind him closely. He feels he has secured a partial victory. The news will travel quickly around the neighborhood: *Marshall was taken down to the police station; he must have gone after Frankie.* This is the message he has been looking for—one of his toughness, of courage. It is the one he wants to broadcast widely.

Walking past the basketball court, Marshall keeps his head up. He is out of sight of the crew on the other side of the street. He cannot tell whether any of Frankie's men have seen him. He makes sure to catch the eye of the teenagers underneath a corroded steel backboard and rim. He feels victorious. Vindicated. Grandpa would be proud.

42

A long line of cars drapes around the corner. One by one, Antoine's crew scampers across the grass, picking up cash, dropping off tiny twenty-dollar bags of dope. Antoine looks guardedly at the customers, especially those he has not seen before. His attitude is that no one who gets high can really be trusted. Yesterday three women, clearly high, tried to run off without paying, which led his team to execute three beatings. The day before, an addict tried to drive away with the team's car, believing the drugs were hidden inside. Every week, the team must respond to a desperate act by a desperate customer.

Antoine liked these incidents to some degree. They enabled his team to pressure test their operations. And they let others see that his team was neither weak nor poorly run.

The last few days have been unsettling. Antoine is worried and unsure about his future. The feeling that someone in a prison cell might be controlling his fate whittles away his self-confidence. The inner compass that he could always rely upon now fails him.

More than ever, he feels the weight of being alone. Solitary by nature, he never needed a strong friendship circle. He was content with Uncle Albert and the parishioners at the church whom his uncle enlisted as an army of caretakers once Antoine's mother grew ill. Over the last few weeks, however, he has felt detached from his uncle—his lifeline. When they meet, Uncle Albert offers a deflated response: "Come pray with me." At this point, the offer feels unhelpful.

The day's traffic is steady and brisk. Antoine motions for Tiny to run inside and check the supplies. If they are running low, he will need to clear away the excess drivers and tell the walk-up customers to return tomorrow.

The setting sun throws down a blanket of frigid air. The customers move quickly to complete their transactions. Huddled up and disappearing inside his fluffy down, Antoine feels anxious and unsettled. Nearly every aspect of his plans has failed to materialize. By this point, he should be heading down the interstate and off to college. Instead, he is the newly appointed leader of the crew, with Frankie nowhere to be seen.

To make things worse, Calvin notified him that the group was likely to be attacked by Mo-Mo, a local rival. "Willie says you got to deal with Mo-Mo before he comes over here," Calvin instructed Antoine. "Go after him. Show them niggers we ain't playing."

Antoine is irked that Willie makes decisions without consulting him. And seemingly without much forethought. Willie should know that this green, inexperienced crew cannot both manage a drug business *and* carry out an organized attack on a seasoned enemy. Each day brings him closer to making a personal visit to Willie, despite the kingpin's insistence that Antoine remain in Chicago.

The remaining customers stuff their dope into pockets and walk away hurriedly. Neighbors' cars return from the afternoon commute and fill the driveways. House lights turn on to give the block a friendly glow. No one takes much notice of the small business that operates on their block each day.

A team member beckons Antoine for an advance on the week's pay. Antoine does not respond. He looks off in the distance. He is thinking about the raid on Mo-Mo. Antoine knows that attacking Mo-Mo, an older gang leader in his early thirties, will be more complicated and dangerous than going after Marshall and his teenage friends. If ever there was a time to quit and take his losses—and probably a beating by Willie's enforcers—now is it.

"We're running low," Tiny squeaks at Antoine from inside the house.

"That's cool," Antoine replies. "Go back inside and close it up. We getting a delivery tonight."

Antoine whistles loudly and the crew stands at alert. The store is now officially closed. Everyone steps quickly so they can head home. One crew member shouts at customers to move away from the house, another heads inside with pockets full of money, and a third cleans up the yard. Antoine looks proudly upon this assembly line. The team hums. But he knows this won't last long.

Calvin pulls up. Antoine sighs and gets ready for yet another unpleasant conversation with Willie's emissary.

"Got to say, you got your shit together, Antoine." Calvin lumbers up the front porch steps, turns around, and marvels at the young men staying focused and following instructions. "You got these niggers in line."

"I hope you told Willie that," Antoine says.

Calvin ignores him and delivers instructions. He will be dropping off weapons for Antoine. "Tonight, you gonna get your delivery. The usual spot. Then, you gonna hit Mo-Mo when he gets his dope from the 59th Street Boys. But don't take his dope. Willie just wants you to scare him a little bit, let him you know you're out there. Maybe drive by and just shoot up in the air. I don't know. Just do *something*."

"*Hmm hmm*," Antoine says with a sigh, continuing to look out past the crew and over to the park.

"Don't do nothing stupid," Calvin said. "You smarter than that."

As he heads down the stairs, Calvin cannot resist a final comment. "Oh, I know you told Frankie to get out of town. And Willie knows too. Don't think you too smart for us, boy! If we want to find him, we will." Calvin laughs, throws out his cigarette on the lawn and makes his way back to the car. His large frame sways down to the car, in time with the stereo blaring out a blues song.

————

Antoine tries to slow down his thoughts as he walks over to see Uncle Albert. He misses his uncle, misses the sound of his voice. Their relationship is strained. Antoine would be happy to receive an angry response—anything other than feeling that Uncle Albert has given up on him.

If he receives a delivery of weapons from Calvin later that evening, he will need to quickly prep the others for an attack on their rival Mo-Mo. *How am I going to get them ready?* he thinks to himself. Training an inexperienced crew seems nearly impossible in such a short period of time—a realization that brings about other unpleasant thoughts. *Maybe I just need to do it myself?* Once again, Antoine realizes he may need to take on more risks than he anticipated.

Antoine spots a small black SUV parked across the street of the church. An unfamiliar man steps out and adjusts his pace to arrive at the church with Antoine.

"Hello, Antoine, I'm your uncle's friend. Okay if we talk?" It is Officer Jerome, dressed not in uniform but in plain clothes.

Antoine says nothing. "What do you say we do our best to get you to college? That's what you would like, no?" Jerome keeps his voice even, and he leans over on the small wooden railing that marks the boundary between the sanctuary of Albert's church and the world outside.

Antoine is at a loss for words.

"To do this, we have to follow a few steps. You'll have to let us help you. If you do that, you'll get your life back. I promise." Jerome pauses. He can see that Antoine is fighting back tears. He doesn't want Antoine to feel any embarrassment—only an opportunity.

"I'm going to find you again, Antoine. Just to keep talking. Albert is not here right now. He wanted you and me to talk. You need to know it's never too late to get on track. I won't say it's going to be easy, but I'm sure me and your uncle can help you find a way. My name is Officer Jerome."

Jerome walks back toward his car. A part of him wanted to make an actual plan with Antoine. But he knows not to push too hard. Antoine needs to trust him before they can work together.

———

Rather than waiting for his uncle to return, Antoine walks off. He heads over to Samir's bodega, picks up some pork rinds, donuts, and Mountain Dew, and ends up at a picnic table by Lake Michigan.

As he watches the waves crash on the rocks, a steady stream of questions plays out in his head. *How am I going to deal with Willie? Should I tell Uncle Albert? When should I let Momma know what's really going on? Should I run away or hide or stay and keep making some money?* Each question comes has its own particular flavor of anxiety.

He is relieved when Missie sends him a message, asking to meet as soon as possible.

Antoine could use a friend. He has already made up his mind. He just needs someone to listen as he declares his intentions.

Antoine wants out. He knows he is at a turning point with Willie's business. If he directs another attack, it will be his second time taking this risk. He was lucky once. After the raid on Marshall's friends, he didn't end up in jail, no one was killed, and the police ignored him. But the next time, he may not be so fortunate. Mo-Mo is sure to retaliate and Antoine is likely to be punished severely. If he survives a beating or shooting, he still has to face the police. All of this will change his status locally—a gangbanger, no longer an aspiring college student who avoided the streets.

Missie pulls up, lighting a cigarette as she walks over and takes a seat on the grass.

"*Ooh!* You look like you late for something. You got *something* on your mind!" she cries out.

"I'm through," he sighs. "I got to get back to what I was doing. I got to get off these motherfucking streets, Missie."

Missie was not expecting this news. She is happy to hear his frustration. She feels the same way about her own life.

"You got a plan?" Missie asks.

"I *had* a plan, but then it got all messed up," Antoine responds, managing to smile.

"You got friends?"

"I *thought* I had friends, but they fucked me over," Antoine says, without a hint of a smile.

"You talked to your uncle," Missie asks.

"He don't really tell me what to do," Antoine says. "Except he sent this man over to see me. A cop."

As Antoine starts to explain his conversation with Officer Jerome, Missie is careful to react with surprise. She cannot let Antoine know that she has been feeding intel to Jerome for years.

"Either you in or out, Antoine. You get it? That's really what you got to figure out first. Maybe your uncle and this cop can help you."

"I'm out."

"Just be careful, you know what I mean—about who you work with." Missie knows Jerome can be trusted, but too much enthusiasm will arouse suspicion.

"No other way out." Antoine shrugs. "What do you know about him?"

Missie offers up a warm show of support. "I hear he helps a lot of young folk around get their lives straight. And I know you're scared. You think someone is gonna kill you 'cause you trying to get out of the game. But you ain't been *in* the game that long, dig? They may say 'Antoine is a little bitch. He couldn't hang with us!' But who cares? You're in college. You're far away from this shit!"

Everything she says seems sensible—and, even better, *feasible*.

43

A half mile away, Frankie holes up in a friend's house a mile south of Rosewood. He will stay in hiding, remaining in the house for much of the day and heading out only at night to get food. Willie is sure to send someone to physically assault him—a punishment for approving an attack on Marshall's friends. Or, as bad, Willie might give him up to the police so he can maintain his sales operations intact. Either way, Frankie has no reason to stay in Rosewood.

Frankie came to this conclusion after speaking with Antoine a few days after the attack. Their conversation was brief. Antoine did his best to persuade Frankie to leave town.

"If you're *here*, those boys got a reason to attack us back," Antoine told Frankie. "If you're *gone*, they probably won't come after us. Which means shit stays quiet and cops don't come around no more. That means we make money and Willie is happy. Get it? If you leave, he's gonna think you made the smart move."

Antoine then gave Frankie the number of his cousin in Iowa City. "Go hide out for a while," Antoine advised the deposed leader. Frankie gratefully accepted Antoine's offer. He realized his future as an earner on Rosewood's streets was over after the shooting.

At least I ain't going back to foster care, he thinks to himself.

44

Missie makes her way over to the row houses to see the squatters. She stops at the small park across the street and takes a seat on a bench. The nearby homeowners and squatters do their best to pick up garbage and maintain a vegetable garden and flower beds in one corner. In another corner, a local junk dealer and street artist has fashioned child-size benches and picnic tables from objects discarded over the years—wooden guitars, window frames, the door of a 1985 Buick, oversize truck tires, and several street signs. A large wooden sign, painted haphazardly in green and white letters, reads, HANDLE THESE KIDS LIKE THEY WERE YOURS.

It has been nonstop reflection for Missie ever since Harpoon asked her to take over the reins. She is tired of wondering if this is a good move for her. A squatter, Otis, spots her sitting at the picnic tables and walks over.

Otis can tell she is bothered. He pushes out smoke through a cheap cigar. "What you need?" he asks.

"What I need only God can provide," she says with a laugh.

"Well, he just sent me over to you, didn't he?" Otis remarks.

Otis is nearly sixty years old, slim, in good shape, and seems ready for the next sixty years of his life. He has been a squatter since his wife and son died in a car accident thirty years ago. He never recovered. Quit his well-paying union job at a textile factory. Drug addiction, a brief stint stealing cars, home burglaries. He never ended up in prison, which he began to interpret as divine intervention. One summer, he decided to give up drugs and stealing, and help out others on the streets. Over the years, with knowledge of how to survive, he has become a mentor for dozens of homeless men on the South Side.

Missie stares at him, envious of his positive spirit. *How can someone who can't even pay rent be so happy?* She laughs.

Missie explains her situation. No point holding back. She confides that she is growing pessimistic about her chances of a different life, one outside the world of gun trafficking.

Otis can appreciate her need for safety and security. He answers slowly, pausing to choose his words with care. "The funny thing about making plans about your life: When you start, you forget that you're figuring out twenty years or thirty! Hard to do that in a *few weeks*. Dig? You could look at it differently and say to yourself, 'I'm taking over from Harpoon to get the time to make my plan.' Stick to it. Dig? And don't quit! Until you're set up to move on."

Missie stares out blankly. She is listening to everything Otis tells her. "Never looked at it that way. Like God giving me a chance to get it all right."

"Funny thing about God." Otis sighs. "He always keeps you guessing. I suppose it helps him to stay interested in all of us."

Otis's voice is soothing.

45

Antoine and his crew wait at the house for further instruction. The drug sales ended two hours ago, there are no customers lingering about, and the neighboring houses are quiet. The team patiently waits as Antoine checks his phone. At any minute, Calvin will send him the time and location for the weapons pickup.

He has started making preparations for a potential drive-by attack on Mo-Mo. *Better to be safe and have a plan*. He called two squatters, asking them to watch Mo-Mo's operations: they will monitor shift changes, when people take breaks, and the busiest and least busy time for customers. Mo-Mo's team traffics their drugs on a small side street. If cars are lined up, or parked on the sides, Antoine may have difficulty making a quick exit. The information from the two squatters will help Antoine plan his attack at just the right time.

He has also identified a pair of his customers whom he will send over to buy drugs from Mo-Mo. He needs to know how well Mo-Mo's team handles unruly situations. Do they seem flustered?

Do they have extra security on hand? Do they bring their guns out when an unexpected situation arises? The customers he sends over will be disruptive—just enough to bring out a response from Mo-Mo's crew.

Calvin finally sends a text, but it is not what Antoine expected. GTS. Their code for "Go to Sleep." The weapons drop-off looks to be delayed.

Antoine tells everyone to go home. He heads over to Uncle Albert's church to move his plan forward. What exactly he will do is unclear, but the refrain echoes through his head. *Got to get out. Got to get out now.*

PART **5**

46

Marshall and Jay drive to the police station, down tree-lined streets dripping with autumn leaves, in silence. In Rosewood, this drive is a ritual. It is one that bonds many fathers to sons who find themselves in trouble. One coming to the aid of the other, lifting them up in a time of distress.

Anger, shame, and gratitude fill Jay's heart as he drives patiently through traffic. He beats himself up for not being there for Marshall. *Maybe things would never have gotten to this point*, he wonders. He knows how fortunate he is that the pastor took charge.

Jay can still feel the protector impulse battling with the feeling that Marshall must take care of himself. *You got to let your son make his own decisions*, he recalls the pastor telling him. For her part, Joycie cares little for the pastor's sentiment or her husband's decision to let Marshall learn on his own. She just wants Marshall to come home, where he'll be safe, where she can cook him a meal.

At the police station, the meeting lasts ten minutes. The officers ask Marshall about the initial Friday night attack. They need to ensure that he understands the seriousness of the situation. Carrying a weapon is not a trivial matter. He did the right thing by turning in the gun, they say, but this doesn't get him out of trouble. They make no promises to go easy on him. Marshall can expect them to call Jay once they finish their investigation. Finally, they urge him to stay close to his parents, remain in school, and forget about the bully. "We're going to be watching you, Marshall," they tell him before saying goodbye.

On the way home, Marshall sends messages to Georgie. *I didn't say nothing, 5.0 couldn't get nothing from me.* Jay looks over at his son and recognizes the sensation Marshall must be feeling. *Honor.* He knows that Marshall needs to hold his head up high among his friends and on Rosewood's streets. He lets Marshall text furiously throughout their ride. Growing up in Rosewood is a tomorrow game, and Marshall has lived for another day.

The weeks are quiet in the Mariot household. Jay and Joycie do their best to rearrange work schedules. They take Marshall to school and pick him up afterward. Principal and teachers keep a watchful eye on him.

The bullying has ended. But Marshall and Georgie are the last known owners of a weapon that might have crimes on it. A few days after the visit to the station, Officer Jerome calls Jay and Joycie.

"It's serious. They got to look a little deeper at that gun. I don't know anything else. That's the best we can do right now," Jerome reports "But your son is alive and in your house right now. Some folks can't say that anymore."

Before this all began, Marshall's chief complaint was the non-stop questioning from his parents, relatives, and local leaders about his future. Now he looks forward to answering those questions.

47

A line of ducklings, mother in tow, marches lively over to the bench. There are plenty of bread crumbs for feeding them at Pastor Jesse's feet.

"Alone or running with someone?" Pastor Jesse asks, zipping up the pouch of food.

"Five years with the local Vice Lord crew," Officer Jerome responds. He zips up his jacket and adjusts his hat. The weather forecast is for a light brushing of snow the first of the season.

"He reach out to you?"

"Missie told me," Officer Jerome responds. "She says he wants out. Says he's a good kid."

"That's a good sign. Better than being a bad kid," Pastor Jesse laughs under his breath. "So, where do we start?" The pastor makes a mental note—this young man could be a candidate for his Book of Names.

Officer Jerome takes a breath. Another story is about to be told. A story of another young man once again brings the pastor and the officer together. It has been a long summer, and it looks to be a long autumn and winter ahead. There's no shortage of teens and young adults in distress, involved in gun violence, and in search of a helping hand.

As for the situation between Marshall and Frankie, they have done all they can do. Jerome sends what he hopes is a final message to Willie: Let your cousin move on with his life. No need for threats. Willie knows that his ability to operate an illegal trade in Rosewood still depends on honoring Jerome's requests.

The pastor's work cannot be wrapped up so neatly. Pastor Jesse's last conversation with father and son repeated the previous exchange—and the one before that. But, the dirty little secret of street diplomacy is that such situations sometimes stay open-ended. Cops, clergy, outreach workers sometimes like to keep a young man like Marshall on edge and worried enough to stay out of trouble. It is likely that neither the cops nor Pastor Jesse will resolve this situation formally, especially if there are no crimes on Marshall's weapon. What Jay and the pastor both know, Marshall likely does not. The police have probably moved on from Marshall.

Pastor Jesse will keep reporting to the family, in Marshall's presence, as he did three weeks after the evening visit to the Mariot home. "Police are still looking into the weapon. We'll just sit tight and wait. Marshall, you should just go about your business. Stay in school, stay out of trouble. . . . Come to church."

48

"I'm going to St. Paul!" Frankie shouts into the phone. The ex–gang leader stands outside a small two-bedroom cottage— Antoine's cousin's house in Iowa City—delivering his weekly up-date to Antoine. For over a month, Frankie has stayed away from Chicago, communicating only with Antoine with burner phones.

The first week was difficult. Frankie kept waking up at night, suspicious of every small noise that he heard outside the window. He kept in touch only with Antoine and used his savings to buy cheap phones from a nearby mini-market. He trusted Antoine. He didn't think that his friend would give up his location to Willie. But he also knew Willie was crafty and creative. Willie would find him if he really wanted to.

To keep busy, Frankie began helping Antoine's cousin, who conducted home repairs in the neighborhood. There was a small group of local young men, a few years older than Frankie, who spent their days riding bicycles or driving around the countryside. They looked up to Frankie, who entertained them with stories of

Chicago's underworld. Frankie liked the pace and feel of a smaller city. The days passed slowly—a welcome change from the pressures and dangers of drug trafficking.

"I got some new friends now," Frankie says proudly to Antoine. "They know someone who got a car wash, in St. Paul. I guess I'll work there for a while. Who knows when I'll come back around your way. Probably never!"

"You sound like you won some money!" Antoine says with a grin. Antoine is surprised at Frankie's chipper, upbeat tone. When they became friends years ago, Frankie was clownish and filled with an innocent deviousness. He lost this energy after his mother passed and he cycled through the foster care system, and then churned through Willie's gang. Despite all they have been through, Antoine is glad to hear the feeling of ease in his friend's voice.

An uncomfortable moment of silence. Neither of them knows what more to say. Antoine breaks up the tension by giving Frankie one more instruction. "Probably best you don't call me no more."

"Yeah, you're right," Frankie agrees. "Talk to you later, maybe."

49

Kennedy-King don't look so bad, Antoine says to himself, standing across the street from the entrance to the nearby community college. He didn't make it to Valparaiso University, as he hoped, but he is on his way. Kennedy-King is only a few miles away from Rosewood, but Antoine feels a sense of wonder. The sights and sounds place in him a distant world. Bicycles, young people walking briskly with backpacks and books, adults wearing suits and ties. No blaring music, no one selling dope, nobody to fear.

Antoine notices that *everyone* is Black. Antoine is surprised, and a little confused. He thought even here, in the heart of Chicago's South Side, higher education would bring a sea of white people.

Antoine stares at the brochures in his hand. He wonders what to ask the college counselor whom he will be meeting in an hour. The technical courses—computer science, electrical circuitry—attract him, as does the program on business. Remaining in Chicago is making him curious about owning a local store—which he had not thought about before. He sees himself managing a number of

SUDHIR VENKATESH

them, spread throughout the South Side—barber shops, dry cleaners, home repair shops. Entrepreneurship feels natural and inviting.

Antoine knows he is lucky to have made it this far. And he has thanked some people for helping him, like Missie. But he knows there are others, most of whom he will never meet again.

Antoine asked Uncle Albert about the role that Officer Jerome might have played. Finally, Uncle Albert relented by providing the barest details. It was Officer Jerome who sent a simple message to Willie: If the kingpin harmed Antoine, Frankie, or any other member of the team, Willie would never be able to work in Rosewood again. Every cop would come down on his street operation.

Hearing this, Antoine made sense of other events. Like his final conversation with Calvin, Willie's emissary. Calvin had called to let him know that the entire sales operation had to be shut down. "Cops are watching" was all that Calvin said. Antoine realizes that Willie acted conservatively. Closing up shop was a smart move to keep the police away and save his drug spot.

And then, to Antoine's surprise, Calvin said, "If I was you, I'd get the fuck out. Willie gonna put a new team in, so this is your chance. If you want to leave, I'll let him know. He ain't gonna stop you." Hearing Calvin's report, Antoine turned around, walked back to the house, and told the rest of his team to go home. He dropped off the remaining drugs and cash to Calvin and then exited the drug trade for good.

Later that night, he stopped by Uncle Albert's church, delivering the message that, finally, he was *out*. It was late, but Uncle Albert requested that they sit and pray. For Antoine, this felt like the most natural thing to do.

"Dear Lord," Uncle Albert said, holding Antoine's hand. "I

272

know we are at the beginning of a long road. You are our driver. We pray for your help with this young man. Will you watch over us as we take that first step, Lord? Will you give us the strength to be patient? Will you keep us safe?"

Two months later, Antoine finds himself here on the Kennedy-King College campus. Not all of his problems have disappeared. If Willie really wants to get him, there isn't much he can do to stop him. But he knows hiding is no longer the answer. And, though his mother is still ill, the doctor's reports show her to be gaining strength. For the moment, it feels better to stay in town, close to her side.

Antoine doesn't want to leave the campus setting. He breathes in the sights and sounds of young people, walking casually and planning their futures. Sipping on a Mountain Dew, he wonders, *How many of these people are like me? How many of them got a second chance?*

50

Missie is running late. She walks briskly across the park and takes a seat on the blanket next to the other women in her team. It is the first weekly team meeting without Harpoon as crew chief. It is Missie's team now. She is in charge.

Her legs feel wobbly. No one is a stranger, but her new role on the team doesn't feel comfortable yet. The others around her are locked into their phones, muttering small talk. She calls everyone to order.

"Should we call Harpoon?" Missie laughs, getting everyone's attention. Harpoon left only a few weeks ago.

"Maybe we put him on speaker and let him yell at us!" Juni says.

Everyone laughs and comes to attention naturally. The rhythm is easy and there is no need for Missie to take a strong hand in what may be the first outfit of local gun traders exclusively managed and staffed by women.

And since taking over, Missie has been counting up the number of women involved in trafficking weapons. Twenty, not including the five on her team. Nearly all the others have been passive operators—either lookouts or homemakers paid to store a gun trader's cache. Only three were involved in executive decisions— handling sales, orchestrating out-of-town gun buys, managing customers and gangs. She can count ten times as many men in the trade.

Missie never thought of herself as setting an example for future generations. She would prefer women not stake their hopes for financial success in weapons trading. But neither is she ashamed of her work.

The conversation with Otis the squatter hums in her head. Until she spoke with him, she looked at her decision to stay in the game as survival. But maybe Otis was right? Giving herself two years to plan an exit is a smart move. She can save enough money to purchase a small apartment in the southern suburbs. She could even invest in her sister's plans to start a beauty salon. *One day, one step ahead, keep it moving*, she tells herself, borrowing a phrase that Harpoon told the team many times to help them focus.

She smiles and sends Harpoon a text as the meeting ends. In the clear, A41, 14A. It is the message they send to each other when separated during an incident of violence or police activity: "We're in the clear, All for One, One for All."

Harpoon replies in seconds. Plain Jane. Missie tells the others, who hoot and holler. Then she heads back home to make lunch for her mother.

51

Three hundred miles away, Harpoon puts his feet up on the porch of his aunt's home. He ended up failing to purchase the small cottage on the street where he was raised—too much cash to spend with a baby on the way. Instead, he took possession of his aunt's two-story bungalow after she passed away unexpectedly. The neighborhood looks much the same—small, filled with Black families.

Harpoon is far from any city, but he is minutes from several transportation corridors in central Illinois—no more than a few hours from anyone who might wish to sell him used weapons. He is not retiring from the gun trade. But he is far enough away from Chicago to change his profile. On occasion, he will distribute weapons wholesale to traders like Missie rather than manage a local operation. The threats will be lower and the pace will be slower. There will be enough business to keep him busy, but he will still have time to raise his first child, who will arrive in a few months.

Every few days, a text message arrives from Pastor Jesse, reminding him that he has another calling—to shepherd young men out of the world of Chicago gun violence.

Harpoon has not forgotten the conversations with Pastor Jesse at his favorite corner bar. He knows that he needs the company of elders. He knows he would be a good foot soldier in the pastor's army of outreach workers who tend to local youth. And, like Missie and Antoine, Harpoon also harbors dreams of investment and entrepreneurship—in his case, a bar back in the Rosewood community or near his favorite street corner on Prairie Avenue.

Looking into the future, Harpoon knows that he will move his family back to Chicago in a few years. Cherise will grow tired of life in a small town and he will need to bring in more income. But, for the moment, he is content. Each morning, he brings his coffee out to the porch to watch a neighboring farmer ride a small red tractor down a stretch of land. Burrowing through the ground, the blades prepare the soil for the winter ahead. The tractor sputters along.

Author's Note

I have been involved on Chicago's South Side for three decades. I have worked with residents professionally, via research studies and documentaries, but they are also my godchildren, friends, mentors, and people I have trained in the use of community-oriented research. To them, I owe a personal debt that I have tried to pay back but know I never can.

This is my fourth book on the South Side. Unlike my previous works, which were community studies, this work focuses on the lives of only a few people. The earlier books used the tools of a researcher, such as sampling and hypothesis testing, and looked at life over years at a time. This book, by contrast, focuses on events over a period of weeks. Though I spent time in Chicago and I spoke to individuals in person and via phone for several years to gather material, this book is a story and is not a work of scientific research intended for academics or policymakers.

This story is the culmination of my thinking over a ten-year period. In 2008, after twenty years of studying crime and poverty in Chicago, I joined the Department of Justice as a senior advisor. I shifted my perspective from the behavior of criminal organizations to law enforcement at federal and local levels. I spoke with cops and federal agents, and I befriended local gun traders, families, and those working in outreach and advocacy. I spent time in parks, bodegas, churches, police departments, street corners, and court-rooms. I left Columbia University in 2016, looking for a story that could bring out this ecosystem in sharp relief. I gathered material for this book between 2016 and 2018, observing and interviewing in and around Chicago.

In this book, there are no composite characters, all events are true, and people who know Chicago will probably guess where (and possibly who) I am talking about. The custom of academic ethnography—which is the in-depth study of small group life—is to change identifiers by giving people pseudonyms, altering locations, and omitting a few details like the exact month and year, that might enable readers to locate people. Like other ethnographers, I make these alterations for two reasons. First, this book is about illegal and risky activity. I do not wish to put people I've known for many years at greater risk. I am humbled that they've let me share their stories, so protecting them is paramount. Second, public discourse on gun violence can make it appear that something is inherently wrong with the people involved or impoverished about their way of life. For over a century, sociologists counter this thinking by empha-sizing situations, contexts, and roles that people play, enabling the reader to imagine individuals acting differently as circumstances change. Adopting pseudonyms is the traditional way social scien-tists motivate readers to focus on the social conditions that give rise to behavior.

I am a trained ethnographer, so observing a small group is not by itself difficult. But most ethnographers look at social life over a period of years to understand underlying patterns. We need time to get at the causes of behavior—otherwise we risk making incorrect inferences from a small sample. This book is an outlier because it traces a single event and the way people make sense of it, in itself a challenge since I was relying on people recalling enough details to help me piece together the story.

To do this, I developed a technique that borrows on a concept called "event history," which anthropologists use to understand the distant past. The past is retained in us via the myths that are passed down from one generation to another. Figure out those myths and you get closer to that past. We often think of myth as falsehood. That's not quite right. Myths are shared forms of storytelling. They are languages that enable people to express their experience—and let others understand them, retain them, and pass them along.

That's why myths are powerful. They are devices that help us get through life, especially when things get stressful, change happens, and/or expectations are not met. In low-income communities, myths are essential tools by which people grapple with the fraught, unstable situation created by inequality, racism, and entrenched hardships like addiction and depression. And they help these same residents create some familiarity and stability by passing down knowledge over time.

My first task, then, was to begin accumulating myths—stories—of gun violence. What was the language people used to share their experiences? Going back to the discussion on roles, I started by asking what myths existed for different roles—parents, youth, cops, gun traders, and so on—in the world of guns. Each role comes with its own style of performance, a distinct use of story to capture and express experience. Parents love to drop the *myth of the gloried past*: "It used to be so much safer in this neighborhood and we used to all get along . . ." Ex-gang leaders turned social workers prefer the *myth of the honorable gang*: "When we were in a gang, we had a code of honor, but now these people will shoot each other for nothing!" Gun traders embrace the *myth of age-appropriate sales* (even though I never once saw any of them ask for identification): "I only sell to people above sixteen."

I used these myths as devices to acquire the perspective of locals on guns. Practically speaking, myths became my starting points for conversation. Signaling empathy and not judgment, they let me create a bond with people. Even though I had been in these communities for a long time, trust cannot be presumed. When I expressed my interest in their myths, people acknowledged it by speaking candidly about difficult issues like guns and violence.

Other pieces fell into place after this, but not always as I predicted. My friend Dorothy ran a small social services agency that mediated gun disputes on Chicago's South Side. Over the past decade, I've helped fundraise for her and other such organizations, and I've observed their work closely. One evening, she introduced me to a gun trader. He and I spoke for two hours. He was anxious because his girlfriend was pregnant. I was a new parent, so we bonded. The next day, he called to thank me and asked if we could talk again. Via phone, we spoke for weeks, sometimes about gun trafficking and other times about parenting. At the same time, I was calling young law enforcement agents, who were busy starting their own families. Despite the differences in our roles and identities, we were all having a set of shared experiences.

I mention this because I learned that my own status as a father would be part of my creative process. Honestly, I didn't want it to be. Initially, I wanted to keep a distance so I would not get too emotionally involved. But—it was too late. I thought about everything with my own kids and wife in mind. Maybe for the first time—and I am a little embarrassed to reveal this—I empathized with just how difficult it was to raise kids in these neighborhoods. And I grew attracted to stories that didn't always land in the media—stories other than the gang shooting or the gun runner caught with a trunkful of weapons. I felt pulled by the families who were just trying to get by, and the kids who just wanted a safe and fun life.

For this reason, the story of Marshall and Frankie stood out for me. I heard of the shooting. And I read the police description, which was brief and perfunctory, and completely inaccurate in terms of reflecting what the incident meant to local families. It was heartbreaking to residents that good-hearted young men kept getting wrapped up in these situations. There was an ecosystem of older people—parents, extended families, teachers, clergy, police officers—doing their best to intervene. But they needed help, more resources—a break in life. I knew it would be more helpful to tell this kind of story since it rarely gets reported in the mass media.

Having identified the event, I started speaking to everyone involved. To bring a single story to life, I initially had people focus on the weeks surrounding the beef between Marshall and Frankie. At the start, this frustrated people. They couldn't easily recall the past. "Why are you asking about the same shit all the time?" they wanted to know.

I realized I was not following my own advice. I began again unlocking their myths. Rather than ask "What happened," I let them guide the conversation by framing it in their own way—with the words and phrases that made sense for them. For example, Marshall never liked talking about the shooting directly. But he *loved* telling me about the pressures of growing up. Senior year was the last year he could be free—hang with friends without all the expectations of parents and family. This frame let him explain why the beef with Frankie was so upsetting—the details about that period in his life then flowed effortlessly. Similarly, Missie found it difficult to recollect details until I asked her to explain what it was like to be a *female* gun trafficker. She loved talking about being a woman on the streets. The frame of gendered labor—the daily discrimination, the expectation to support her household, the need to mentor other women in the trade—similarly freed her up and unlocked her speech.

As one can imagine, it became challenging to piece together the event from all these myths, stories, and remembrances. That task was my responsibility, and mine alone. I patched together that time period as accurately as I could given each person's unique perspective.

Acknowledgments

I am indebted to a countless number of individuals, some of whom have been with me since my early days of fieldwork in Chicago in the 1990s. So few scholars and writers ever obtain the privilege of telling someone else's story. Imagine being included, supported, and welcomed for three decades. How could one ever match that gracious gesture?

I begin at the beginning.

My journey into Chicago's gun world started when I spent days and nights with Dorothy, Autry, and others working at Services at the Door—an informal group that Dorothy and Autry set up to heal the victims of the city's gun violence. They let me ride along with them, through Chicago's South Side. I watched them mediate disputes, support families, and help young people deal with emotions that overwhelmed them. This book principally comes out of a decade of observing them do God's work. I owe a special debt of gratitude to Beauty Turner, a spirited reporter and community organizer who passed away at fifty-one years of age. Beauty inspired so many youth to take a more positive direction, and she kindly introduced me to Pastor Watkins and Pastor Lucas—self-described shepherds of local youth. Thank you all for watching my back.

In another part of the city, I learned by observing Teny Gross and the staff at the Institute for Nonviolence Chicago harness the teachings of Martin Luther King Jr. and the perspective of nonviolence to heal those impacted by gun violence. Always eloquent and passionate, Teny has been an influential source of wisdom as I put this book together.

I am indebted to all my team members at Facebook who helped me to understand the intersection of digital technology and youth violence. Matt Katsaros and Pete Fleming became my teachers and dear friends, and this book couldn't have been written without their support.

Jens Ludwig and Phil Cook, the brightest minds and the most trusted sources on gun markets, encouraged me to find my voice and taught me the complexities of national gun policy. Sunil Garg, Matthew McGuire, and Baron Pineda read early drafts of this manuscript, as they have done for my other books. When I felt lost, they helped me get back on track. Ben Mintz provided encouragement and insight from the first to the last draft. An author himself, Ben kept me honest to myself and the community. Faculty at Harvard's Kennedy School of Government encouraged me think about ways to make this work accessible, and Tracey Meares and her students at Yale Law provided valuable feedback for some formative ideas.

This is my third book with my agent, Suzanne Gluck, an unending voice of support and encouragement. This is my first book with my editor, Sean Manning, who lifted me up repeatedly with brilliant insights, editorial guidance, and kindness.

Judy and Robert Millner welcomed me into their family, and I will always be grateful for their love. My parents, Alladi and Uma, and my sister, Urmila, were with me the entire journey, including a brief respite in Silicon Valley, where the seeds of this book were sown. I must thank my father, especially, for encouraging me never to give up writing, wherever I sat.

My wife, Amanda Millner Fairbanks, wrote her first book while I prepared this manuscript. As she crafted *The Lost Boys of Montauk*, I found myself peering over her shoulder, amazed at her capacity to channel her passion into words on a page. Watching her compose taught me to be a better writer. I am grateful for her love and encouragement.

This book is dedicated to my children, Theodore and Violet. They often ask me about Chicago, and how and why I ended up there. I tell them I was looking for America and I found it in the Lady by the Lake. I hope they find their own place in this country, and never stop learning by journeying into other worlds.